FRACTAL TRADING

· ·

BOOK ORDERING INFORMATION AT END OF BOOK

All praise, honor, and glory be to God –
the LORD God Almighty, the Lord Jesus Christ

FRACTAL TRADING

Analyzing Financial Markets
using Fractal Geometry
and the Golden Ratio

Soul Esprit

Servant of the Lord Jesus Christ

NarrowGate Publishing

Fractal Trading: Analyzing Financial Markets using Fractal Geometry and the Golden Ratio

Copyright © 2011 Soul Esprit
Published by NarrowGate Publishing

All Scripture verses quoted are from the Authorized 1611 King James Bible.

ISBN: 978-0-9841281-6-7

Library of Congress Control Number: 2010941893

Second Edition 2014

CONTENTS

Give glory to the LORD your God, before he cause darkness, and before your feet stumble upon the dark mountains, and, while ye look for light, he turn it into the shadow of death, and make it gross darkness.

– Jeremiah 13:16

PREFACE

This book is an advanced study of an effective approach for predicting future price changes in financial markets. It assumes the reader has at least a cursory familiarity with technical analysis known to be utilized in the industry for gauging market price behavior. Except for basic arithmetic computations, no other technical knowledge or mathematical skills are required.

Some of the concepts and trading techniques presented in this volume were originated by the author. Others are widely known and are implemented by those who trade or invest in financial markets. For the ideas selected to be included in the overall strategy there has been applied a more comprehensive understanding or sharper focus in order for them to more fully integrate with the precision requirements of the author's Fractal Analysis.

This concise brief work provides specific instruction that will enable those who understand and can apply these concepts to forecast market direction and anticipate the character of future price movements.

INTRODUCTION

All naturally occurring phenomena exhibit an *ordered structure*, a repeatable form based on identical or nearly identical subunits making up the whole. This "self similarity" appears to be God's preferred way of structuring physical systems and organizing the material universe into a stable and *ordered configuration*, one that can quickly adapt to *predicable chaos*.

God's perfect order is evident in all of His creation, on every scale: from the subatomic atom to mega-clusters of galaxies. Throughout the seemingly infinite universe there exists certain mathematical relationships characteristic of physical systems; a design evident, for example, in minute electron orbitals or the universe of planetary and galactic systems. The distinguishing features of God's perfect order can be directly observed in the repeated pattern sequence of the outline of a leaf, silhouette of a tree, mountain range, or an aerial view of a shoreline. It can also be seen in a population growth curve: the natural life cycle of growth, maturation, and death. When a graphic representation is made of energy dissipating physical systems, a similar pattern emerges. For instance, a shock wave, voice print, or an oscilloscope tracing of a heart beat. Each of the above shows a characteristic upward advancing energy pulse terminating in a peak, which soon abruptly declines to approximately the initial level. This is a typical bell-shaped curve well known to science, and illustrates a pattern common to all time-dependent phenomenon. To the untrained eye there may seem to be no discernible design evident in the previously mentioned examples, yet, hidden within the apparent chaos is a subtle order manifested at every level, even to the minutest degree.

It has often been said that "history repeats itself." Since natural laws created by God operate on a reoccurring principle, there is built-in reliability for predicting the subsequent design of any naturally occurring system. Consequently, it is possible to determine, often with amazing precision, the eventual completion of an incomplete cycle. Because most cyclical time-dependent events exhibit basically the same intrinsic design character when plotted graphically, once that character is understood, it becomes possible to anticipate the subsequent time-related outcome of future events.

When illustrated graphically, an economic cycle, such as demonstrated by the Dow Jones Industrial Average (DJIA), is a representation of a standard growth curve and is similar in design to the other periodic functions previously mentioned. In aggregate, the U.S. stock market, or any broad-based financial market, represents the sum total future aspirations and fears of a large number of individual stock investors; the price data is a visual illustration of the collective opinions of the divergent group from which it was compiled. Price oscillations are therefore not a meaningless chaotic jumble, but rather, a concise summary of *mass human expectations* regarding the future. It is highly organized information with an implicit order and underlying meaning.

Applying God's implicit design to an historical record of any large capitalization financial market reveals a certain degree of reliability for accurately predicting the future direction of that market economy. Repeatable cycles are evident in all time frames: from one minute intervals to periods spanning centuries of price data. The long-term economic cycles coincide with business expansion and contraction, and with few understood exceptions, the basic design character remains constant throughout boom times and depressions, inflationary and deflationary periods, wars and recessions. When viewed from a limited timeline perspective, any naturally-occurring system illustrates a configuration that is merely a subunit of a comprehensive whole. Only when larger segments of the structure are taken into consideration does a more integrated picture emerge. Without a reference starting point it is impossible to discern any predictive meaning to the overall pattern.

Apparent chaos found in the natural world is subject to an underlying order and predetermination. Future events are unfolding according to God's intrinsic laws. Large Stock Indices and broad-based financial markets such as the DJIA, S&P, NASDAQ, Gold and Bond markets, have historically provided a predictable summary of the past, present *and future* of those markets. Therefore, the forces governing financial markets are *not* random unpredictable chaos, but *are expected* to occur predicated on certain design parameters, and it is God that establishes the parameters. Since the Creator of the universe, Jesus Christ, is not a God of confusion, but of order, therefore, the ultimate future emergent design is knowable.

Chaos Theory predicts a widely divergent outcome when initial parameters are altered. This is called the Butterfly Effect. Any *fundamental* approach to anticipating future economic trends is radically altered by even *slight changes* to the initial conditions. This can be seen, for example, in the limited accuracy of weather forecasting, where small changes in the initial conditions produce large discrepancies in the outcome of longer-term events. Therefore, a rigid, static approach is inherently limited and will produce inaccurate results. Only a dynamically changing systematic procedure can account for variations and unexpected causal factors affecting the eventual outcome. For this reason it is mere speculation for economists to forecast the future course of economic events, since constantly changing conditions insures the initial state will "spontaneously shift" to yield a wrong conclusion. Typically, their opinions prove to be incorrect, and, at best, are bad advice. To the dismay and frustration of many, the upward or downward movement of financial markets, and the U.S. stock market in particular, is not always a direct function of external events. There is often no observable relationship between political or economic news and the subsequent direction in which the market will react. This is because these events are not the antecedent, but rather, the consequence of a pre-existing determination established by the rule of God, not by the rule of man. The future pattern already existed.

In conclusion, identifying where the market price is located at any point in its long-term cycle provides an unique perspective of the future course of any exchange traded market. To illustrate the past, present, *and future* of that market, one needs to first recognize the *implicit order* evident in the apparent random chaos created by the collective investing public. This can be seen in large stock indices and other financial or commodities markets with a sufficiently large open interest of investors to create a volume of buyers and sellers for a balanced and fair marketplace. Although much economic data is collected and analyzed by economists seeking to describe the future production, management and distribution of American and global resources, such a tedious approach has not only proven to be inaccurate, but is also unnecessary. This is because *fundamental data* is always incomplete and often subjective, and therefore leads to erroneous conclusions. Consequently, the approach taken by economists and other modern-day soothsayers hoping to foretell the future is inadequate for describing the destiny of any large market or national economy. This daunting task is greatly simplified by an understanding of the intricate fractal design of God's perfectly ordered universe.

1 COUNTING FRACTALS

In the 17th century, mathematician and philosopher Gottfried Leibniz studied recursive self-similarity in order to describe a mathematical foundation as the basis for the formation of fractals. In 1872, Karl Weierstrass produced a graph that was everywhere mathematically continuous but no where differentiable. This established the groundwork for the definition of a fractal.

The term "fractal," derived from the Latin word "fractus," meaning "broken" or "fractured" (i.e. "fragmented"), was coined in 1975 by Benoit B. Mandelbrot (1924-2010). The phrase "fractal geometry" was used by Ralph Nelson Elliott (1871-1948) in reference to what later came to be known as "Elliott Waves". During the 1930's Elliott was the first to identify a consistent structure evident in the price movement of 30 stocks comprising the Dow Jones Industrial Average. References to "financial market fractals" later came into vogue by prominent academicians, among whom was Mandelbrot, who originated his ideas relative to Fractal Geometry from the work of his predecessor, R.N. Elliott. However, Mandelbrot was skeptical regarding the predictive value inherent in counting fractals, ascribing a degree of uncertainty to what he considered to be the "subjective judgment of the chartist."

Fractal Geometry, grounded in objective scientific observation, characterizes an ordered sequential configuration seen in many natural and computer-generated phenomena. It is a descript term for quantifying the self-similarity structural properties of naturally-occurring physical systems. The phrase "Fractal Analysis" was originated by the author to describe this structure in relation to other features of his methodology. The geometric fractal aspect of the subsequent study is based on the work of Leibniz, Weierstrass and Elliott, as well as the discovery of Leonardo de Pisa and ancient Greek mathematicians. The author adds his own understanding of the fractal concept, and incorporates original elements into the overall analysis that clarify parameters which previously elicited criticism by skeptics such as Mandelbrot and modern day technical and fundamental analysts. Once Fractal Analysis is mastered, it provides the fundamental basis for a highly accurate means to predict future price movements in financial markets, as well as other time-dependent studies.

No *man* invented Fractal Geometry. God did. As to its discovery – it was always there. All one need do is look at God's magnificent creation: observe a leaf or a snow flake, the clouds, a mountain range, lightning bolts, trees and their branching limbs, systems of blood vessels and arteries, river networks, seismic fault lines, crystals, coastlines, and even the lowly cauliflower and broccoli – fractals are everywhere. Romans 1:19-20 further elucidates: *Because that which may be known of God is manifest in them; for God hath shown it unto them. For the invisible things of him from the creation of the world are clearly seen, being understood by the things that are made, even his eternal power and Godhead; so that they are without excuse.* Fractal Geometry is a concept having predictive value because it is an expression of the Creator God, Jesus Christ (John 1:1-3; Revelation 19:13; Revelation 1:1,2), Who never changes (Malachi 3:6; Hebrews 13:8). For this reason it *will* unfold according to the *fractal configuration*. All that is written in the 1611 King James Bible Word of God is prophesy; God spoke it (2 Timothy 3:16), and whatever He speaks, He creates (Genesis 1:3,6,9,11,14,20,24,26,29). On any time scale, from the subatomic minutiae to infinity itself, there is a divine order to God's creation because He literally spoke it into existence. Therefore, since he has spoken His Word (and written it in His 1611 King James Bible), His plan for this world will not fail, but *must* come to pass.

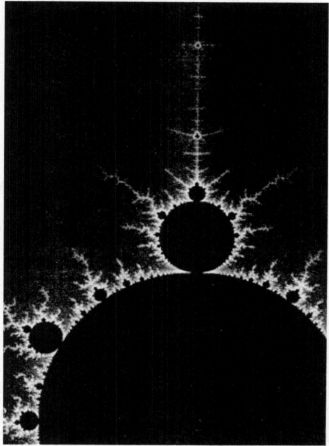

**The Mandelbrot Set illustrates fractal
characteristics to a seemingly infinite degree.**

The basis of the fractal configuration is "self-similarity." The
overall structure consists of repeatable subunits characterized by
an encompassing symmetry. Each subunit contributes to the formation of a larger degree unit, which is itself a subunit of a still
larger degree unit. In the encompassing aggregate, the whole re-
sembles each of its derivative parts. Naturally occurring systems,
including price movements in financial markets, can be graphically illustrated by a perspective overview of how the subunits relate
to formations of higher degrees. Figure 1 is a simplified example.

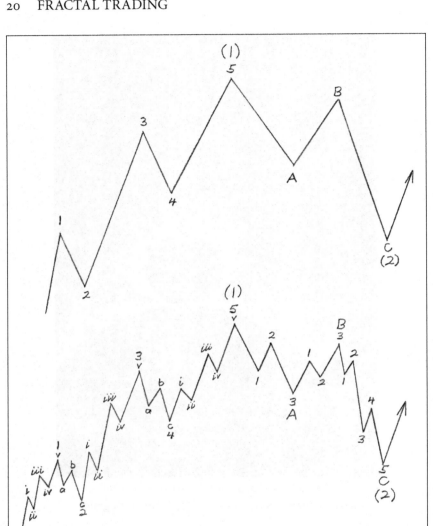

**Figure 1. A typical fractal pattern showing
3 degrees in an advancing market.**

The 5 - 3 configuration is evident in advancing markets or declining markets. Whereas an up or down 5 sequence indicates the direction of the prevailing trend, an up or down 3 fractal sequence is always corrective. Figure 2 illustrates a fractal sequence in a declining market.

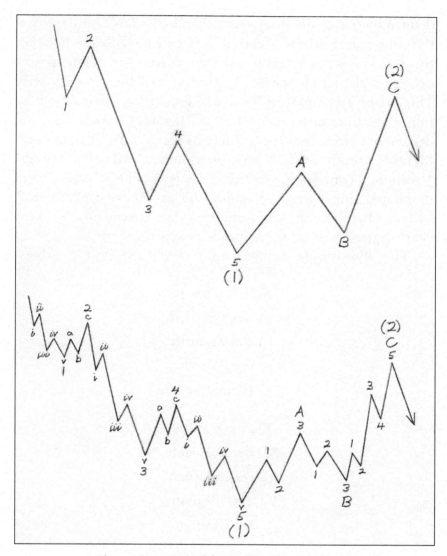

**Figure 2. A typical fractal pattern showing
3 degrees in a declining market.**

A 5 - 3 formation appears at each stage in building the larger 8 movement structure. (ref. Appendix C for fractals counting in groups of 3's, being the exception to the rule.) At every degree is seen this same basic design, yet, the degrees are not always defined by size or duration, but rather, by *form* – i.e. subunits of the same degree may be of entirely different size and duration. For this reason it is important to maintain perspective of any specific degree by relating it to the next larger degrees of the overall pattern. This can be accomplished by maintaining price charts for all the important time intervals of the market under consideration. In descending order, these time intervals include: Yearly, Quarterly, Monthly, Weekly, Daily, Hourly, 30 Minute, 15 Minute, 5 Minute, 1 Minute. (Time frames less than Daily should be charted and monitored only if greater precision entries and exits are required, such as when trading short-term intra-day movements.) For each chart degree, the Fractal Analysis is exactly the same.

The following are charting time intervals used by the author:

All Data/Yearly

10 Years/Quarterly

2 Years/Monthly

1 Year/Weekly

3 Months/Daily

10 Days/Hourly

5 Days/30 Minute

2 Days/15 Minute

2 Days/5 Minute

1 Day/1 Minute

The serious analyst will have saved in the computer, real-time automatically updated charts for each of the above time frames. Ideally, he should have 5 computers, each monitor allocated to one of the 5 key *trading* time intervals: Daily, Hourly, 30 Minute, 15 Minute, 5 Minute, (alternate: 1 Minute); each screen with in-stant access to 2 tab windows, each tab containing a stored chart: one showing price bars in candlesticks, the other indicating price format by open/high/low/close (OHLC). The analyst should also maintain print out copies of the Daily through Yearly charts in order to have available for quick reference on clipboards an updated hard copy of the overall Analysis, including the Fractal Count, as well as other studies soon to be discussed.

Another important facet of the 5 - 3 subunit configuration is its propensity to become more complex over time. This is a pronounced tendency seen with further development of each subsequent fractal within the same degree of the larger structure. In the top pattern illustrated in Figure 1, the second and third iteration pattern would be expected to take on increasingly greater complexity than the first movement, resembling the progressively subdivided fractal sequences of 5 - 3 shown in the diagram directly beneath it.

Complexity can be expressed as a *continuation* of an ongoing fractal pattern, or by adding smaller degree fractals. A 5 fractal extension subdivides by units of 4. Thus, 5 increases to 9; 9 to 13; 13 to 17; 17 to 21, etc. Likewise for the corrective mode: 3 increases to 7; 7 to 11; 11 to 15; 15 to 19, etc. On the Daily chart, the most commonly seen continuation subdivision in the direction of the prevailing trend is 9 or 13; for the Daily chart corrective trend, subdivided continuations are typically 7 or 11. Smaller time frames may show further continuation subdivisions.

As depicted in Figure 1, for an *advancing* movement in the 5 - 3 trend direction, the first advance is Fractal 1, labeled F1 or simply 1; the first counter movement to F1 is Fractal 2, labeled F2 or 2; the next advance is Fractal 3, F3 or 3; the movement counter to F3 is Fractal 4, F4 or 4; and the final advance is Fractal 5, F5 or 5. The subsequent 3 fractal correction of the F1 - F5 movement consists of Fractal A, labeled FA or A for the first counter movement; followed by a counter move to FA: Fractal B, FB or B; and lastly, a counter movement to FB: Fractal C, FC or C, which completes the larger degree (F1) to (F2) 8 fractal sequence. As previously mentioned, 5 fractal subunits can continue to include 4 additional component subunits consisting of 9, 13, 17, etc. Likewise, the 3 corrective fractals can continue in form to create a larger more complex subunit configuration consisting of 7, 11, 15, etc. The labeling rules are the same for *declining* 5 - 3 movements, as shown in Figure 2.

From highest to lowest degree, the following is a suggested convenient labeling system for designating fractal degrees. The reader is free to devise their own numerical designations, and may utilize more degrees, if needed (e.g. underlined or circled degrees).

[F1]	(F1)	F1	fi
[F2]	(F2)	F2	fii
[F3]	(F3)	F3	fiii
[F4]	(F4)	F4	fiv
[F5]	(F5)	F5	fv
[FA]	(FA)	FA	fa
[FB]	(FB)	FB	fb
[FC]	(FC)	FC	fc

Or, simplified:

[1]	(1)	1	i
[2]	(2)	2	ii
[3]	(3)	3	iii
[4]	(4)	4	iv
[5]	(5)	5	v
[A]	(A)	A	a
[B]	(B)	B	b
[C]	(C)	C	c

When initiating a starting point for the Fractal Count, always begin with the Yearly price chart. The analyst should first examine the long-term price data in order to identify the largest degree of the 5 - 3 fractal configuration. Once that has been achieved, further analysis will reveal 5 - 3 subunits within the larger 8 movement framework on the same chart, as exemplified by Figure 3.

Upon completing the smallest degree evident on the Yearly chart, transfer that labeling sequence to the next shorter time interval, which is Quarterly. Starting from the largest transferable degree, successively label degrees down to the smallest degree possible on the Quarterly chart. Then transfer that data to the Monthly chart, repeating the process for price charts of Weekly, Daily, Hourly, etc.

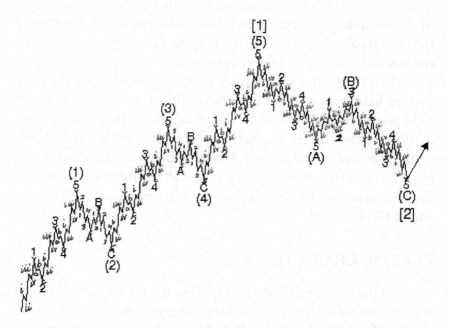

Figure 3. Idealized conception of the fractal pattern showing 4 degrees in an advancing market. Note the repeating 8 subunit sequences throughout the overall fractal configuration. This illustration could depict any time frame chart – from 1 Minute to Yearly or Decade price bar intervals. A 3 Fractal Count in the trending direction is atypical, but can occur (ref. Appendix C).

The objective of Fractal Analysis is to *project* future price movements according to the basic fractal pattern shown in Figures 1 through 3. But remember, the pattern illustrated is an *idealized form* not always seen in the unfolding configuration in real time. This is especially true on the shorter-term time intervals less than

Daily. Often, the idealized form is distorted and warped to such an extent that it is unrecognizable as the standard fractal pattern; only the subunit count remains intact. For this reason it is of paramount importance to carefully inspect and compare price bars with preceding and subsequent time interval charts, scrutinizing every detail of the pattern as it unfolds in real time in order to correctly label all 5 - 3 fractal components. When changing from one time interval chart to another, any omitted price bars will result in compounding error for anticipating subsequent development of the fractal pattern. Being "off" by just one price bar may invalidate the fractal count for all lower degree charts.

When the fractal subunits are correctly labeled, and the price pattern has been projected into the future for a sufficient duration to be useful for the analyst, he then has a powerful means to predict where the current market price is located within the overall comprehensive fractal pattern. Utilizing that information, trading positions can then be opened or closed at key junctures – such as the completion of F2, completion of F4, termination of F5; or the end of FA, FB, or FC.

FRACTAL CHARACTER

Certain rules can be applied to describe the characteristics of each fractal subunit within the larger degree pattern. While these are specific rules, they *generally* hold true and are not *always* reliable for price movement predictability. Further, especially due to the massive influx of traders and institutional investors utilizing preprogrammed computer algorithms, these rules sometimes require modification such that the astute analyst must be aware of any exceptions to the rule.

F1: Usually the shortest in extent. May not subdivide. Or, if breaks down into smaller fractal constituents, may count as 3 subunits rather than 5.

F2: Typically long relative to F1. Will often retrace .618, .809, or .854 the distance of F1. When short, will be in the range of .500 - .146 the length of F1. (The derivative 1.618 Golden Ratios: .854, .809, .618, .500, .146, etc., will be discussed in Chapter 3.) It is possible on occasion for an F2 correction to exceed the full extent of F1, correcting 100 percent, or more, of F1.

F3: Frequently the longest movement of the 5 fractal advance or decline, but sometimes will be surpassed by a continuation F5, and much less often by the length or duration of F1. The second iteration (e.g. fiii of F3) or larger degree, e.g. F3 of (F3), will typically subdivide into smaller subunits which may further subdivide – e.g. fiii of F3 of (F3) of [F3]; each third fractal iteration tending to be the longest subunit within the respective comparative degree. In extremely rare instances, F3 will be the shortest among the 3 trending fractal movements.

F4: In price charts of larger degree movements (Daily, Weekly, Monthly, etc.) the fourth fractal is typified by a protracted period of sideways advances and declines. The termination of F4 often retraces approximately 50 percent of F3, which is usually to the level of lower degree f4 of F3. If F4 is extremely shortened, it will stop at the next lower degree fourth fractal, i.e. fiv (ref. Chapter 2/Diamond Count/second chart). The character of F4 can be used to anticipate the character of subsequent F5. For example, if F4 retraces more than 50 percent of F3, F5 will usually be short relative to F3; if F4 is shorter than 50 percent the retracement of F3 (i.e. .382, .236, .146) F5 will likely be as long or longer than F3. Especially in shorter-term time interval charts, it is possible for F4 to overlap with F1, but typically, this is not the case.

F5: Can be either long or short relative to F1 and F3. Is infamous for extending the trend long past what is expected by support/resistance levels and momentum Confirming Indicators (Chapter 5). The Alternating Principle (Chapter 2) can be used to great advantage when comparing the character of previous F5's of corresponding degree.

FA: Begins the downward corrective phase (or upward corrective phase in a decline) of the 5 fractal sequence advance (or decline). Can be either short and simply constructed, or long and subdivided. Typically breaks down into either 5 or 3 subunits of smaller degree.

FB: Always comprised of 3 fractal subunits, which may further subdivide to form 7, 11, etc. Since it is essentially an F2 correction of FA, it will often react strongly against the FA countertrend and may occasionally exceed the terminal extent of F5. When FA is in a fast momentum corrective move (5 subunits), FB tends to be short relative to FA. Comparing the unfolding FB to FA, the Alternating Principle can predetermine the character and length of FB.

FC: Because this is the third movement, it is essentially an F3 fractal, and thus is often the longest and fastest movement of the ABC 3 corrective fractals. This third leg will typically unfold with less subunit complexity than either FA or FB, and should be labeled 5 fractal subunits, or, if a continuation trend, 9, 13, etc.

At least one of the 3 major fractals in the direction of the prevailing trend (i.e. 1, 3, 5) will be a continuation; the remaining one or two fractals will be of a less complex configuration. Alternatively, all three trending fractals may subdivide to form continuation patterns, especially the smaller degree subunits in a larger degree terminal fractal 5 movement. Overall, two of the three trending movements will be of approximately the same length and duration – either shorter or longer than the comparison fractal. This could be F1 and F3, F3 and F5, or F1 and F5.

General rules regarding the impossibility of F1/F4 overlap and F3 never being the shortest among the three fractals in the direction of the prevailing trend are incorrect. Especially as seen in shorter-term time frames (1 minute - Daily), overlap and relatively short F3's do indeed occur, and with sufficient frequency to invalidate any suppositions to the contrary. In highly manipulated markets, such as Gold or the Stock Indices, F2 and F4 can correct 100 percent or more of F1 or F3, respectively.

Summarizing: The objective of Fractal Analysis is to identify where the price is located within its patterned sequence. By doing so, it is possible to anticipate not only the direction in which the price is next most likely to move, but also the precise timing, speed, duration, and character of that movement. The author's method approach allows for multiple confirmations of key turning points – not relying exclusively on the Fractal Count – with the consequent ability to anticipate establishing market positions *before* the former trend has changed direction. In order to successfully negotiate this maneuver, the analyst must have attained a mastery of the basic fractal concept, as well as a practiced understanding of all other aspects comprising the author's Fractal Analysis. (By itself, the Fractal Count is insufficient for timing market turns.) That methodology will be further developed and defined in the subsequent chapters to follow.

2 THE ALTERNATING PRINCIPLE

When utilized in the context of Fractal Counting, the Alternating Principle is the most important and versatile concept presented in this book. A thorough understanding of its multi-faceted application will render market price behavior transparent and enables the astute short-term trader or long-term investor to position in advance of significant price movements which otherwise could not have been anticipated. The Alternating Principle applies to nearly every aspect of the comprehensive Analysis: the Fractal Count, Confirming Indicators, Fractal Character, Comparative Fractals, analogous fractal movements of different time frame charts (e.g. Weekly vs. Daily), etc. It confers a significant advantage by enhancing the degree of predictive value in forecasting future price projections.

The Alternating Principle involves comparative analogous (same degree) fractal subunits demonstrating the *opposite* or *alternating* characteristic of their corresponding equivalent. For example, if corrective (F2) is short, expect corrective (F4) to be relatively long. If F1 of (F3) is short and constructed of a *simple* one bar for its otherwise constituent 5 subunits, the corresponding F1 of (F5) will tend to be either relatively long, and/or will be of normal length but *complex* in its structure, forming a continuation movement in at least one of the 3 trending subunit fractals. Likewise, if F2 of (F3) was long (.618, .854 of F1, or longer), expect F2 of (F5) to be relatively short. Always keep in mind that corresponding fractals do not repeat in the same manner.

Extremes in range are compensated for by an opposite extreme in the corresponding fractal movement. For example, if F5 of F(3) formed a long continuation sequence of smaller degree subunits, there exists a high probability that F5 of (F5) will be extremely short, or even aborted.

The previous examples are illustrated by the following chart:

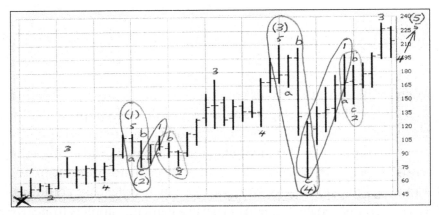

Uniformity in the constituent fractal pattern is made possible by the Alternating Principle. Note the (1)/(4) overlap that corrected more than 100 percent of (3).

Price continuations are subsequently compensated by elongated counter-movements, or by shortened or aborted corresponding analogous fractal subunits. This compensatory mechanism is evident at every level of fractal comparison.

When applying this useful tool to price charts it is important to realize that the Alternating Principle will sometimes "shift" when comparing the same price area between different time frame charts. To illustrate, if (F2) appears long on the Weekly chart, it may appear shortened on the 5 bar Daily chart. Likewise, a short F3 of (F5) on the Quarterly chart may appear to be considerably longer on the corresponding 3 bar Monthly chart. This discrepancy is a result of how the changing prices "roll over" to the comparative time interval chart. Since price movements do not "know" when a particular time frame has begun or completed, there is often a carry-over to the subsequent bar. The analyst must be aware of this phenomenon and allow for its occurrence by diligent comparison of price bars between different time interval charts.

Further application of the Alternating Principle is seen among the supplementary Confirming Indicator studies (Chapter 5). Confirming Indicators exhibit the tendency to alternate, as do comparative price bar openings and closings. For instance, if an analogous fv of F3 closed near the height of its extent, expect the corresponding fv of F5 to close near the low of its price range. If there was a sudden price gap at the market opening of an fiii of F1, expect the fv of F1 open to be flat or down.

The analyst should be cognizant of the reality that the Alternating Principle is always in effect. Provided that the Fractal Count has been correctly applied, tremendous advantage can accrue when positioning in advance of an expected price reversal. As a further example, a shortened or aborted F5 at the termination of FA in a 3 fractal large degree correction would almost invariably yield a long continuation F5 in the subsequent FC. For a final illustration, an F5 of (F3) that is shortened or aborted should in the subsequent corresponding F5 of (F5) produce the converse character of continuing the fractal configuration into lower degree subunits long past what is anticipated by support/resistance studies. Having advance knowledge such as this, and the confidence to act on it, could produce substantial returns or preserve capital by knowing to either sell early or not take a position in a market that was expected to quickly reverse direction because the comparative fractal was an exceptionally long continuation movement exceeding support or resistance levels anticipated by other aspects of the Analysis.

THE DIAMOND COUNT

This is a concept devised by the author to simplify assigning values to price bars whenever encountering a potential continuation trend that defies a conventional fractal count. Should there be a series of what appear as the same degree subunit fractals, without an expected trend change (e.g. F2 or F4 correction), it is sometimes convenient and useful to group lower degree fractals into a single larger degree, observing the basic rules of fractal counting. This may help to clarify the true count and facilitate making comparisons between and among analogous fractals for subsequent application of the Alternating Principle.

An example of where the Diamond Count could prove beneficial is shown in the following charts. To illustrate, the first chart shows a fractal count where larger degree (2) is approximately the same length as the constituent corrective subunits comprising (1). Likewise, (4) appears to be excessively shortened, in violation of the Alternating Principle. This false count can be reordered by labeling the first fractal subunit Diamond 1, and the seventh subunit Diamond 3. As shown in the second chart, the subsequent counter movement will then become Diamond 4; with a terminal ninth subunit continuation move in the direction of the previous trend, labeled Diamond 5. By making this adjustment, the overall configuration conforms to the characteristic fractal pattern.

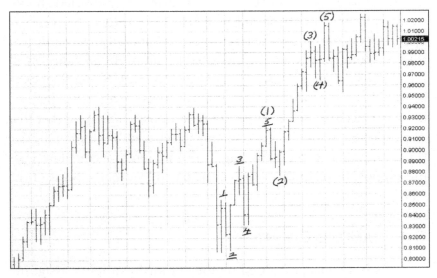

This ambiguous Fractal Count is clarified by a revised Diamond Count (next chart) that will facilitate subsequent fractal comparisons using the Alternating Principle.

The Diamond Count elucidates a more characteristic pattern in each of the advancing 3 fractal movements.

The advantage conferred by the Diamond Count can be realized by comparative observation of the fractal character as it develops in real time. Should the analyst become aware of a basic flaw when counting fractal degrees in the early stages of a directional price trend, and while applying the Alternating Principle, he should consider the possibility that a continuation move is in progress. Applying the Diamond Count will help to anticipate the configuration of the next price fractal based on the Alternating Principle.

The Diamond Count has further application in determining whether a price pattern is in the direction of the prevailing trend or is corrective in nature. Counting price bars in the ongoing movement will often make this clear, but sometimes only after the major trend or correction has been completed and confirmed by other studies. The following chart shows this type of Diamond Count clarification.

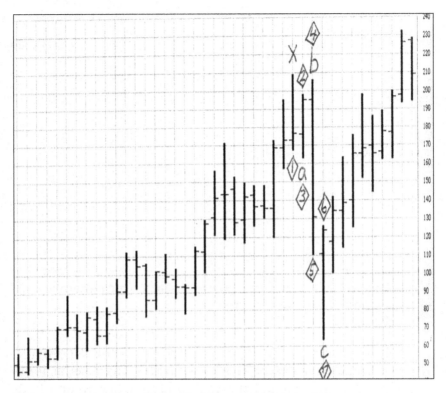

A Diamond count may simplify determining whether movements are part of a prevailing trend or corrective in nature. This chart shows a 7 subunit three fractal ABC correction.

Once a terminal reversal point has been established for the first of subsequent larger degree fractals in the new trend direction, the Alternating Principle can then be applied for gaining insight into the structure of subsequent advances and declines.

The Diamond Count provides other advantages besides those mentioned here, and is a general application tool that may be utilized in short or long-term charts. It can serve as a visual aid for maintaining the overall characteristic fractal configuration by bringing into clearer focus the "big picture" which otherwise might be overlooked when dealing in smaller degrees.

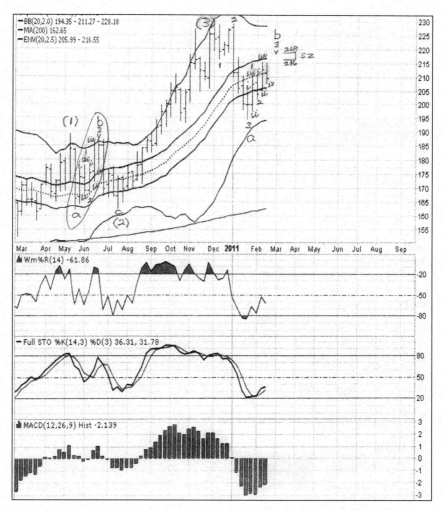

Weekly chart comparing b of (4) to b of (2). Alternating Principle evident in 2 and also v3 b of (4), anticipated to be relatively long compared to v3 b of (2); b of (4) is expected to be short compared to b of (2).

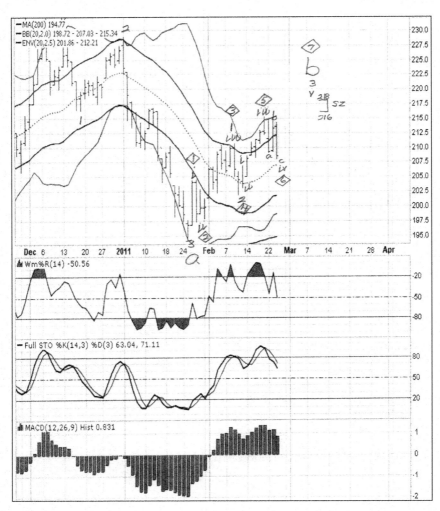

Daily chart of same movement showing a Diamond Count clarification of b.

3 THE GOLDEN RATIO AND FIBONACCI SERIES

The Golden Ratio – also known by other names such as Golden Mean, Golden Section – was discovered by the Greeks who incorporated it into their art and architecture. Often denoted by the Greek letter, Phi, the mathematics of the Golden Ratio are evident in many forms and configurations found throughout the natural world. For example, it can be seen in a microscopic strand of double helix DNA, or a macrocosmic system as large as a spiral galaxy.

Although it has not yet been formally proposed in the scientific literature, the author's belief is that the structure of the entire galactic universe is a fractal based on the Golden Ratio. (The Frontispiece of this book, opposite the Title Page, shows how the distribution of matter throughout the universe might appear from a vantage point beyond space and time.)

The Golden Ratio is derived by a fractional subdivision of a unit measure. Illustrated below, Figure 4 shows this mathematical relationship:

Figure 4.   /_____A_____/_____B_____/

The ratio of B to A + B is equal to the ratio of A to B.

$$\frac{B}{A+B} = \frac{A}{B} = \frac{1}{1.618}$$

The value of the Golden Ratio is calculated by:

$$\frac{1 + \sqrt{5}}{2} = \frac{1}{1.618}$$

The derivative .618 decimal is the inverse of the Golden Ratio:

$$\frac{1}{1.618} = .618$$

The Golden Ratio is generally regarded as 1.618; .618 is its reciprocal. This Ratio is evident in the Fibonacci Series, which consists of the following progressive infinite number series:

1, 1, 2, 3, 5, 8, 13, 21, 34, 55, 89, 144, 233 ...

Each number is the product of the previous two numbers. This summation series relates to the 1.618 Golden Ratio or its .618 inverse. The following fractal decimals are derived from the 1.618 Golden Ratio, its .618 inverse, or their derivatives: *.146* (= .618 x .236; .382 x .382), *.236* (= .618 x .382; .146 x 1.618), *.382* (= .618 x .618; .236 + .146), *.500* (= 1.000/2.000), *.573* (= .382 x 1.500; .500 x 1.146), *.809* (= .500 x 1.618), *.854* (= .618 x 1.382; .618 + .236), *1.000* (= .618 x 1.618; .618 + .382), *2.000* (= 1.618/.809), as well as several other decimal ratios of lesser significance to Fractal Analysis. (There are more arithmetic ways to derive the above ratios than what has been shown.) Whole numbers combine with the .618 Ratio and its derivatives to form numbers important to the Fractal Analysis study, e.g. 1.618, 2.618, 3.618 ... 1.145, 2.236, 3.382, 4.500. These ratios are derived from the inverse of the .618 Ratio or its derivatives, e.g. 1/.618 = 1.618; 1/.382 = 2.618, etc.

The following table shows the relationship of the Golden Ratio to numbers in the Fibonacci Series and the number which precedes it:

First Number	Second Number	Ratio
1	1	1.0000
1	2	2.0000
2	3	1.5000
3	5	1.6667
5	8	1.6000
8	13	1.6250
13	21	1.6154
21	34	1.6190
34	55	1.6176
55	89	1.6182
89	144	1.6180

When considering *fractal price analysis*, the most commonly used ratios are .618, .500, .382. For example, the primary retracement levels of corrective F2 are .618 and .500; for F4 the most common retracement levels are .500 and .382. There are other applications of the Golden Ratio and its derivatives that can further define the fractal price structure. For instance, the study of *fractal time analysis* can be utilized to project turning points at specific times in the future unfolding fractal pattern. Golden Ratios applied to key time intervals – e.g. anticipating significant tops or bottoms – often yield accurate price levels at which subsequent reversal points will occur. Expected future price areas determined by such fractal time analysis are confirmed by the Fractal Count, fractal price analysis, Confirming Indicators, and support/resistance Golden Ratio Arcs and Trendlines, next to be discussed.

GOLDEN RATIO ARCS
AND TRENDLINES

The 1.618 ratio and its derivatives can be applied to forecast projected price movements. The DJIA chart below illustrates the accuracy of this ratio by the use of a compass to draw *Golden Ratio Arcs* for anticipating and confirming the fractal price pattern. The unit measure is based on the distance from the start of a trend change to the start of the first major correction. Note the price penetration of the arcs.

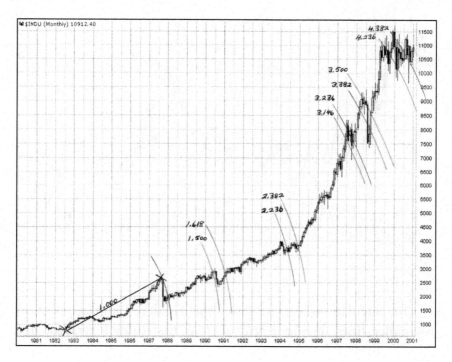

Golden Ratio Trendlines are useful for projecting support and resistance levels, as demonstrated in the below charts of the U.S. Dollar Index. Future turning points based on the key ratios can be identified far in advance.

To calculate where to draw the Golden Ratio support or resistance lines during a *price advance*, first draw a straight line connecting the highest and lowest points of a significant decline. Next, draw a parallel line using the highest corrective high of the decline. Measure the distance between the two parallel lines, label as 1, then multiply this value by whole numbers of key Golden Ratio derivatives, as shown below. (It is best to draw many lines, rather than few, in order to define the entire movement.) Note how the lines pre-signal both terminal advance *and* decline areas.

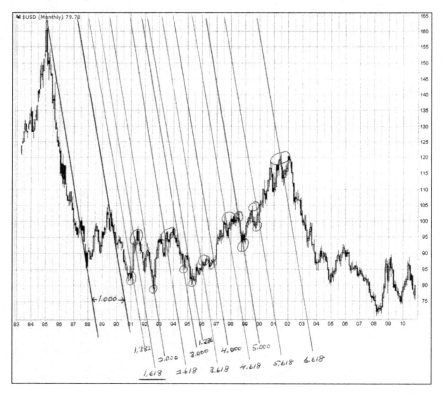

To calculate where to draw the Golden Ratio support or resistance lines during a *price decline*, first draw a straight line connecting the lowest and highest points of a significant advance. Next, draw a parallel line using the lowest corrective low of the advance. Measure the distance between the two parallel lines, label as 1, then multiply this value by whole numbers of key Golden Ratio derivatives, as shown below.

When combined with a correct Fractal Count, Arcs and Trendlines are an effective means for capturing the entire movement as it unfolds. Certain of the Ratios selected by the analyst will not be relevant as key turning points for the larger degree fractal, but may coincide with smaller degree subunits within the overall structure. Convergence of Trendlines with Arcs can be useful as an aid when assigning values to the Fractal Count. The Arc and Trendline study can be drawn either before or after a numerical Count has been determined.

FAST ZONES

When used together, support and resistance Golden Ratio Trendlines form a grid characterized by open areas resembling a diamond or parallelogram structure. Upon crossing into a new zone, the price often moves to extremes of the range defined by the grid configuration.

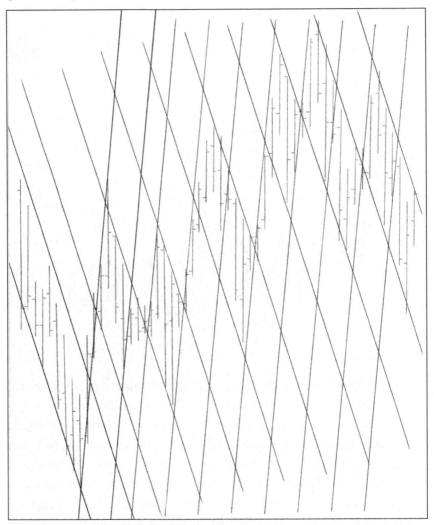

Golden Ratio support and resistance Trendlines create "Fast Zones" where prices tend to move at accelerated speed.

5   CONFIRMING INDICATORS

Without a correct Fractal Count, technical indicators are of limited value, and can be of no value, or even negative (loss) value. For this reason the Fractal Analysis is heavily weighted in favor of a correct Fractal Count: approximately 80%/20%. If the Fractal Count is incorrect, just the converse is true, and the Fractal Count is subordinate to the other technical tools: approximately 20%/80%. The Analysis is most effective when both the Fractal Count and the Confirming Indicators are correctly understood in relation to each other.

When considered in isolation, the Fractal Count can sometimes appear to be unclear. In order to narrow the possibilities for a true count, it should be confirmed by the use of certain other analytical means besides Fractal Arcs and Trendlines. The following supplementary indicators provide additional confirmation for the trend direction, and can also serve as an aid to identify where the current price is generally located within the overall 5 - 3 configuration. Today there are more than 50 technical indicators available on the open market, but most of them are inconsistent or conflicting. In the author's experience, the following select indicators have proven to be the most reliable, especially when used in conjunction with each other. Implementing too many technical indicators produces a null result and is detrimental for confirming or arriving at a true Fractal Count. It is therefore not advised to add to or subtract from those Confirming Indicators discussed in this chapter.

% R

Also known as Williams %R, this is a gauge of momentum strength which oscillates between a high above 20 and a low less than 80, with a bisecting midline of 50. It is usually set at a period of 14 bars. Compared to the other Confirming Indicators, %R provides an *advance notice* of when a particular time frame has *potentially* reached its maximum extent and is about to turn. Buy and sell signals are indicated by a breakout from the extremes of the oscillator ranges, but false signals are often generated. (Notice the several false signals in the first half of the below illustration.) %R movements should be tracked using Fractal Counts, which often mirror and confirm the price movement and can help clarify a price count that seems uncertain.

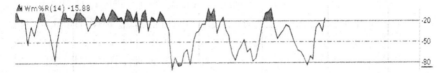

RSI

The Relative Strength Index is also a momentum indicator, and ranges between a high above 70 and a low beneath 30, with a bisecting midline at 50. It is one of the indicators most favored by technical analysts, and, like %R, is calculated in 14 bar intervals. Also similar to %R, RSI movements can be tracked using Fractal Counts.

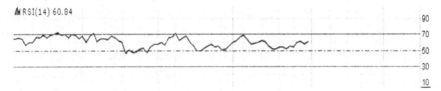

STOCHASTIC

This momentum gauge oscillates above a high of 80 and beneath a low of 20. Unlike the above indicators, it uses two lines which cross at the extremes or 50 midline range. Calculated for periods of %K

(14,3) and %D(3), Stochastic will provide confirmation of a trend *continuation* when the previous two indicators are beginning to signal a *turning point* (i.e. %R and RSI have generated a short-term *false* signal). A buy or sell signal is indicated by line crossings at the extremes of the oscillator range, but may also be signaled at the midline. There are both slow and fast stochastics; to filter out false signals, Full Stochastic is preferred.

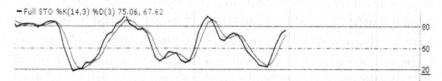

When considered together, the above 3 momentum indicators provide an added level of confidence for labeling the Fractal Count.

MACD HISTOGRAM

This indicator should be considered independently of the above momentum indicators since it may contradict some or all of them at any given time. Measured in 14 bars, it is commonly seen in relation to the Moving Average Convergence/Divergence (MACD) technical indicator, and for that reason is often overlooked. Since it provides a nonarbitrary visual assessment of market direction, it is used to best advantage as a stand alone indicator apart from the MACD. For the Swing Trader whose trading interval is measured in terms of 1 to 3 weeks, the key time frames where the Histogram proves most effective are the Daily and Hourly charts. Shorter bars on the Daily interval generally indicate an approaching short-term top or bottom in the current price direction. The trader should prepare to exit his position somewhere between the first registered shortened bar and the cross-over at the midline range. (But shortened bars are not *always* conclusive, and can be a false signal, especially when not mirrored by the Fractal Count.) Once the bars have made the transition to the up or down side of the bisecting midline, the second indication of a trend reversal has been confirmed. But until that point is reached the reversal is not confirmed, as seen in the below example where shortened bars did not always immediately progress to a midline crossing, and thus, a significant price change of direction. The same rules apply for the Hourly Histogram that will give notice of a trend reversal for *corrections* during a sustained Daily advance or decline. These crossover points usually represent times at which a position can be exited for a profit or additional positions can be added. When implemented in conjunction with a correct Fractal Count, the MACD Histogram false signals can be filtered out and better interpreted. Failure to act as soon as a confirmed signal is generated will sometimes result in being on the wrong side of the market in a fast F3 breakout.

It must be stressed that although these particular momentum indicators may be helpful in discerning support/resistance levels and future price direction, they can be misleading if not understood within the framework of a correct Fractal Count. The astute analyst needs to be aware that oscillators and trading ranges are of limited value and cannot be relied upon as an independent tool, but must be seen in the larger context of the overall Fractal Analysis. When taken out of this context, Momentum Indicators and levels of support/resistance *do lie*. For this reason, they are not to be trusted without additional supporting confirmation. In order for these supplementary indicators to have any validity for successfully gauging future price movements, they must be seen in relation to a correct Fractal Count applied to *all key time frames*. When implemented in proper balance, the Confirming Indicators and Fractal Count mutually confirm each other.

REGRESSION TO THE MEAN

A Sine Wave follows the basic Fornier Transform showing wave oscillations that are useful for musical engineering and other commercial or scientific applications. It demonstrates the statistical concept of Regression to the Mean, showing constant time frequencies oscillating above and below a midline within a minimum/maximum range. Both, price movements and the 4 previously mentioned momentum Confirming Indicators exhibit Sine Wave characteristics.

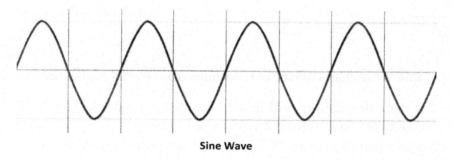

Sine Wave

An advantage of envisioning the price as an oscillating Sine Wave function is that it identifies where the current price is located in relation to certain other volatility measures such as Bollinger Bands, Moving Average Envelopes and Moving Averages (discussed below). When these are superimposed over a price chart they create a structural framework for gauging relative highs and lows within an oscillating range of price fluctuations. For example, key Moving Averages such as 18 bar, will often bisect superimposed Bollinger Bands to provide a framework for a relative price reading at any point during a price advance or decline. When further adding the MA Envelope, an additional level of support and resistance encapsulates nearly the full range of any price movement.

Regression to the Mean is a statistical concept describing the tendency for equal probability events (e.g. equal amount of capital invested by sellers and buyers) to gravitate toward a statistical norm or average of those events. Price changes in financial markets show this Regressive tendency, and can therefore be viewed as a Sine Wave function of Fornier-like design.

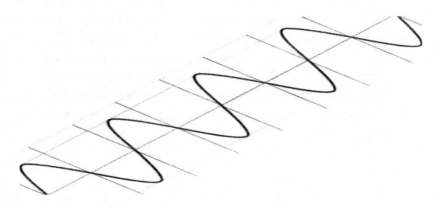

Sine Wave characteristic of the 8 movement fractal configuration

Price fluctuations within a directional 5 or 3 fractal trend will exhibit the characteristic form of a Sine Wave moving at constant speed when passing above and below a bisecting midline that connects the starting and terminal points. Illustrating wave oscillations, a Sine Wave pattern describes the basic fractal configuration evident in price movement oscillations seen below:

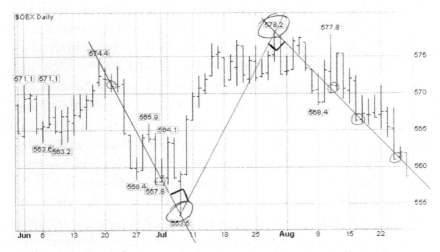

Trading window of opportunity: Some markets generally cycle every 2-3 weeks. Within this time frame it is possible to make a profitable Swing Trade.

Volatility can be measured in terms of identifying trading ranges of the price movement. The following are three means by which that can be accomplished.

BOLLINGER BANDS

This price range gauge provides a visually objective basis for identifying the price relative to support and resistance levels, and has its greatest utility when used together with other aspects of Fractal Analysis. Typically, F3 and/or F5 will touch the upper level band during a terminal phase of an advance, or the lower band during a terminal decline. Bollinger Bands also serve as an aid to confirm price projections based on the Fractal Count and Golden Ratio Arcs and Trendlines.

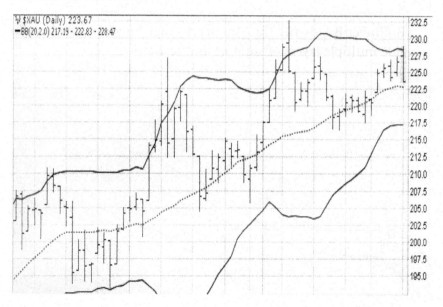

MOVING AVERAGE (MA) ENVELOPE

This volatility reading compliments price support and resistance levels identified with Bollinger Bands by providing an additional level where advancing or declining prices are most likely to react.

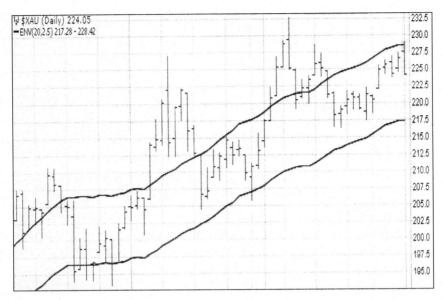

Bollinger Bands and the Moving Average Envelope combine to provide multiple layers of support and resistance:

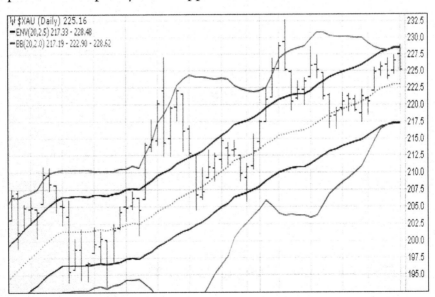

MULTIPLE MOVING AVERAGES

Key Moving Averages complete the price overlay of the support/ resistance framework. The important moving averages are 18, 50, 200, as measured in terms of price bars for any of the time frame charts. Subunit fractals within a correct Fractal Count will often coincide with these Moving Average price levels.

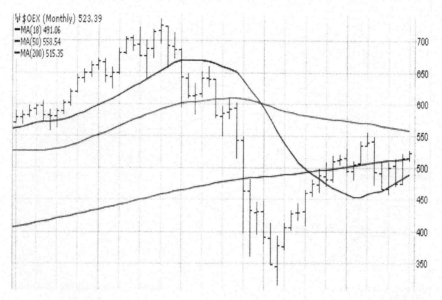

By adding Moving Averages to Bollinger Bands and Moving Average Envelopes, the analyst has a visual guide for anticipating when the market has moved to extremes of investor optimism or pessimism. When key Moving Averages are superimposed over the above 2 volatility channels, a visual field is created to further identify areas of price reaction.

Combining all of the above Confirming Indicators creates a price chart that looks like this:

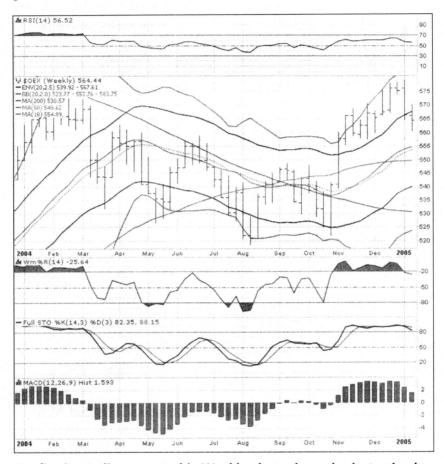

Confirming Indicators on this Weekly chart show the last price bar is part of a correction in a continuation uptrend. Support levels are between 555 - 550.

6

TRADING OPTIONS, STOCKS, FUTURES, FOREX

Without the benefit and advantages of the Fractal Trading methodology outlined in this book, the author strongly advises against speculating or investing in any type of financial market. The rigors implicit in the endeavor are such that any other approach is inadequate for the task and will invariably encounter difficulty and potential for financial loss, or perhaps even total ruin. With the advanced information provided by correct application of Fractal Analysis, nearly all fairly operated markets can be successfully traded or held for a profitable longer-term duration.

To follow is a commentary on four different financial instruments for participation in financial markets. Some of these investment vehicles offer certain advantages not available to others. Depending upon one's trading experience, degree of expertise, and level of capitalization, these investment vehicles may or may not be suitable for some investors.

OPTIONS

The largest option index markets are the Standard and Poor's 100 (OEX) and NASDAQ (QQQ). The high trading volume and open interest of these markets makes them ideal candidates for timing price movements using the fractal analytic methodology. Smaller markets generally do not lend themselves well to the study, and this is why the author recommends trading large volume/large open interest Option Indices rather than individual stock options or options on small capitalization Futures. (There are other large options indices beside OEX and QQQ.)

Options consist of two components: Time Value and Intrinsic Value. The first reflects the amount of time remaining on the purchased Contract Month; the second is relative to the price as it approaches or penetrates a specified price level known as the Strike Price. Positions can be taken for either side of an option market: *Buying* (Purchase) of Calls if the expected market direction is upward; *Buying* (Purchase) of Puts if the anticipated price direction is downward. When implementing a Straddle approach, simultaneous Puts and Calls can be held, but often to disadvantage because of the price/time erosion factor. (The time value of an option does not decrease in a linear constant loss manner, but rather, during the last few days before expiration, the time value depreciation *increases at a faster rate* since there is less uncertainty about the probable market value of the underlying market asset.) Options expire on the third Friday of each month. In the Futures markets, option expiration is the third Thursday of each month.

Selling (Writing) Calls or Puts works the opposite of *Buying* Calls or Puts. Option Sellers (Premium Sellers) hold the other side of the contract for the Option Buyer (Premium Buyer) contract purchase. When an investor Sells Calls, he is expecting the market to decline, and thus collect the premium paid by the Call Buyer if the underlying market price fails to penetrate above the Call Strike Price by the option expiration date. When Selling Puts, the investor is expecting the underlying market price to advance, and thus to collect the premium paid by the Put Buyer if the underlying market price fails to penetrate below the Put Strike Price by the option expiration date. Premium Sellers take on a greater degree of risk than Premium Buyers, since Buyers may only have a portion of their total capital at risk, whereas a Seller has potentially all of his invested capital at stake to cover a trending market moving adversely to his position. For this reason, Option Writers are required by their brokerage firm to be substantially better capitalized than Option Buyers.

Among the four types of investment vehicles discussed in this chapter, the most favorable risk/reward ratio is achieved from Buying Index Options according to the Capital Management strategy outlined in Chapter 7. When implementing Fractal Analysis within a Swing Trade time frame interval of 1 to 3 weeks, leverage is generated while limiting the option time erosion factor or overpaying at the time of option purchase. With this approach it is possible to accrue significant profits measured in terms of appreciating option premium. Double and even triple-digit returns on open positions within a 5 day market week are realistically attainable for those market technicians with the expertise to maneuver in a rapidly changing price environment. In addition to sudden price volatility for compounding invested capital, options have the further advantage of reducing downside risk. Whereas total or near total capital loss is potentially possible for Option Writers and when trading Futures, Forex or Stocks, purchasing Options limit losses to the amount of capital committed to an open position. This fact provides an intrinsic advantage when short-term Swing Trading, since the potential for gain is virtually unlimited, while the possibility for total loss is restricted to the fractional amount at risk in any given trade position. This favorable mathematical ratio allows for using relatively small amounts of capital to generate proportionally massive profits during a brief interval of time. The arithmetic advantage is exemplified by the following:

Double 1 cent 10 times = $10.24

Double 1 cent 20 times = $10,486

Double $100 10 times = $102,400

Double $500 10 times = $512,000

Double $10,000 10 times = $10,240,000

Alternately double then triple $100 10 times = $1,555,200

Alternately double then triple $500 10 times = $1,728,000

Alternately double then triple $1000 10 times = $2,592,000

By the use of Options it is possible to yield a multiple of invested capital within a brief period of time, usually during the Swing Trading parameter of 1 to 3 weeks. Occasionally, a doubling of capital, or greater, can occur in a single day, or even in a matter of minutes. Therefore, the above figures are realistic when applied to this highly leveraged investment vehicle. For this reason, and because of the limited downside risk potential of trading options, the ratio of risk to reward is relatively small compared to other types of trading vehicles, such as Futures or Forex. Option trading allows for cash reserve capital to be used to add more positions should new entry opportunities become available during the course of an existing open trade. In this manner it is possible to leverage a small amount of capital into a much larger sum within a compressed period of time (ref. Appendix D). Trading Options using the author's Fractal Analysis and Capital Management Strategy can be a profitable entrepreneurial venture for the small or large investor. As a safeguard against loss, buy the nearest Strike and always purchase at least *4 months of time value*. (Successful Premium Sellers sell 4-6 weeks of time value because they know most option contracts subtantially depreciate or *expire worthless* during that brief time interval.)

STOCKS

There is little that needs to be said about short-term trading or investing for the long-term in the stock market. Essentially, the price at which a stock is purchased becomes the base level price for measuring any subsequent gains or losses. For example, if a stock is bought at a price of $10 per share, it will have to increase to $20 per share in order to produce a doubling of the position price. This can sometimes require years to occur, or it may never transpire. Unless implementing a Margin Account (which doubles the potential risk), there is no leveraging factor as when trading Index Options, Futures, or Forex. Stock price movements are a one to one price/profit correspondence: a $1 movement up or down produces a net $1 per share gain or loss. Like the other three trading vehicles discussed in this chapter, stocks can be "shorted" to generate profits during a price decline. Yet, stock brokers and the brokerage companies they represent do not encourage short selling among their clients, primarily because it is "Bad PR."

FUTURES

Unlike when trading Options, a Futures position can only be established for one side of the same market (long or short) at any given time. If attempting to simultaneously short and go long in the same market, positions will offset each other to yield a net long/short position, depending upon the number of contracts purchased for each side of the market. (Establishing a second futures account with the same or different broker would obviate this inherent disadvantage.)

Futures are traded on Margin of up to 97 percent of the investor's account value. While this provides a considerable interest-free cash flow advantage, it is only beneficial as long as the traded market is moving favorably to the investor's position. In an adverse move it becomes a double-edged sword, rapidly accruing losses. During a price move counter to an established position, should there be too little Maintenance Margin in the account to offset the paper loss, the speculator will receive a Margin Call from his clearing broker demanding additional funds be added to his account in order to cover the balance deficit and bring it up to the level of the Initial Margin requirement. If the trader fails to comply in a timely manner (Margin Calls are sometimes on short notice, triggered within minutes of an adverse move creating demand for more capital) the broker will unilaterally commandeer his client's account, selling off as many open positions as needed to cover the Initial Margin deficit, and always incurring a realized loss for the client. Soon after the forced sale, the market may react to have recovered the intra-day loss, but it will be too late. As to whether or not this state of affairs is planned sabotage to rid the investor of his funds is open to discussion. Yet, with sufficient well-timed frequency of occurrence, it eventually becomes obvious that the investor has acquired a "loose cannon" for a "business partner," an individual working at an institution that has no concern for whether the client makes or loses money, but only cares if he generates commissions for the brokerage firm; and whose sole interest is protecting his company from loss. A broker issuing a Margin Call does not have his client's best interests at heart.

Most Futures Brokerage firms have a minimum required account size that can range from $1000 to $10,000. But realistically, unless an investor has initially funded his account to six figures (preferably mid-range) this choice of trading vehicle can be a losing proposition, and – due to Margin Requirements, price manipulation and targeted stops – can be the proverbial "sucker's game." In the author's opinion, the only "safe" way to participate in the highly leveraged Futures markets is to not use Stop Loss Orders, be properly capitalized to at least 5 times the Initial Margin Requirement for each market being traded, and to set mental stops based on Fractal Analysis.

Among the largest Open Interest Futures Markets are U.S. Bonds, S&P 500, Corn, and several of the Currencies, such as the Euro and Japanese Yen. Futures Currency Markets are "Spot Markets," not "Cash Markets," like Forex Currency Markets. The smaller the market, the greater the likelihood for competing Commercial investors to sabotage a speculator's position by taking a larger counter position to artificially move the price in their desired direction and thus induce losses for the speculator. Smaller Futures Brokers will also use this tactic, especially if they are Locals physically present on the CBOT Trading Floor, with the resultant setting off Stop Loss Orders (Stops) that repeatedly frustrate a trader's attempts to establish a position. If you are going to use Stops, do so with the full understanding that those on the trading floor can see your stop orders and set them off, at will. This becomes particularly important in the futures markets, where buy and sell stop orders are known by the floor brokers and the stop can therefore be penetrated to execute a buy or sell order just before the market turns to resume what could have been a profitable trade (... *the love of money is the root of all evil.* - 1 Timothy 6:10). Bottom line, they *cheat*.

Futures traders should have an inventory of at least 7 tradable markets to chose from. (Due to extreme insider price manipulation, not all futures markets are tradable using the author's Fractal

Analysis.) Profits should be used to purchase more contracts, but do not over buy. At least 50 percent of the total capital should be maintained in cash reserve at all times. Contracts should be sold to free up capital in order to avoid a Margin Call that could occur at a less opportune moment. Suspend trading whenever half of the investment capital has been lost. Evaluate mistakes made in the Fractal Analysis; apply further study to the methodology before deciding whether to resume trading at a later date.

FOREX

Forex Contracts are actually short-term Futures Contracts, but without some of the negative aspects of Futures trading. Futures Currency Markets are not Forex Markets.

Unlike Futures, there is no Initial or Maintenance Margin required for trading on the Forex exchanges. But the rule is that a loss of greater than 80 percent of the total capital in one's account will require the broker to liquidate positions. Therefore, as with trading Futures, one is shackled to a rogue "business partner," and at considerable "extra charge."

The Leveraging Factor in Forex is generally between 1 to 100, but can range anywhere from approximately 50 to 1, and 200 to 1. For example, $1.00 controls $100; $1000 controls $100,000; $10,000 controls $1 million. This works fine as long as markets move favorably to an open position, but if positioned on the wrong side of a fast moving market, it is possible, and likely, to essentially get wiped out.

The Forex Exchange (FX) Market, also known as the Cash Currency Market, is traded in currency pairs. Some of the most popular Forex markets involve the U.S. Dollar Index (USD). There are other currency pairs based in other currencies, such as the Euro, British Pound, or Japanese Yen. For example, GPB/JPY, EUR/JPY, EUR/GPB. The minimum unit size is called a "Pip". The following is a list of the 8 most traded Forex markets. The first symbol in the pair is the Base Currency, the second symbol is the Quote Currency.

Forex Market	Symbol	Street Name
Euro vs. U.S. Dollar	EUR/USD	Euro
Great Britain Pound vs. U.S. Dollar	GBP/USD	Pound, Sterling, Cable
German Deutche Mark vs. U.S. Dollar	DEM/USD	Mark
Australian Dollar vs. U.S. Dollar	AUD/USD	Aussie
New Zealand Dollar vs. U.S. Dollar	NZD/USD	Kiwi
U.S. Dollar vs. Swiss Franc	USD/CHF	Swissie
U.S. Dollar vs. Japanese Yen	USD/JPY	Yen
U.S. Dollar vs. Canadian Dollar	USD/CAD	Loonie

In descending order, trading volume for the above 8 Forex markets are as follows:

Market	Percentage of total Forex Exchange
USD/JPY	17%
GBP/USD	14%
AUD/USD	5%
USD/CHF; USD/CAD	4%
EUR/USD; DEM/USD; NZD/USD	< 3%

The following is a list of some advantages of trading Forex verses Futures:

1) Markets are open 24 hours/5½ days per week (mid-day Sunday to Friday).

2) Electronic Order Execution (no "middleman" pit).

3) No Broker Commissions.

4) Leveraging factor of 1 to 100, or more.

5) Daily Forex volume (1.9 Trillion contracts) is 60 times larger than daily NYSE volume (320,000 shares), and 500 times larger than total Futures market volume (40,000 contracts). Therefore, Forex has lower volatility and less price manipulation.

6) No "Slippage"; guaranteed Stop Loss.

7) No "Up Tick Rule."

8) Due to large Open Interest volume, Forex currencies tend to *trend longer* than some other markets because of less market manipulation. This fact lends itself well to a technical approach.

THE PSYCHOLOGY OF TRADING

Unless trading a very short time interval, it is best not to keep too close a watch on intra-day market activity. If maintaining a tick-by-tick watch on price action, you will bias your previously derived objective analysis that was made from a detached perspective when distanced from the moment by moment subjectivity of observing real-time price changes. An otherwise effective trader can yield to pressure when the market is temporarily moving against his position. By ignoring intra-day "noise" the experienced trader spares himself the anxiety of reacting every time the market registers a counter tick on short time interval charts. For this reason, from a psychological perspective, it is often more advantageous for the trader to defocus from the intra-day picture of what any particular market is doing, and instead concentrate attention on longer-term time interval charts.

If properly derived, the analyst's original Fractal Count is more likely to be the correct interpretation of market price movement as it unfolds. Attempting to change the Count configuration when subjected to the pressure of intra-day price volatility carries a higher probability for error than price/momentum considerations after the close of the market when all price activity has ceased for the day. The best analysis, with the greatest likelihood of accuracy, is obtained when not currently holding an open position, or when not directly focusing on a particular market. When "defocused" and nothing is at stake, the analyst's objectivity is optimized, and his bias will be at its lowest point.

Do not be in too much of a hurry to begin your sojourn in trading or investing in financial markets. It is a highly technical skill that requires at least 6 months of Fractal Analysis study and paper trading practice before one is prepared to use real money. If your paper trading results are not generating consistent profits, neither will you have success when risking capital in a brokerage account. Test the Fractal Analytic methodology throughout the extended time period of remaining in paper trading mode. Unless you have attained proficiency to at least the 70 percent level of trade accuracy on paper, it is unwise to proceed using real money.

FURTHER APPLICATIONS OF FRACTALS AND THE GOLDEN RATIO

A fractal study finds application in diverse non-financial areas such as medicine, soil mechanics and seismology, mathematics, scientific research, and observations of social and cultural trends. In the field of art, several Renaissance painters such as Leonardo da Vinci made use of the Golden Ratio in their work to create the illusion of depth perspective. The .618 Golden Ratio derivative is evident in proportional measurements of the human body and spiral galaxies. Geometric fractals and mathematical Golden

Ratios are seen in Greek and Roman architecture. Modern day construction engineering also incorporates these same universal geometric principles. Time-plotted events characterizing sociological historic trends reveal an integrated picture of human behavior. If a fractal study is applied to public sentiment of optimism versus pessimism, for example, there emerges a graphic representation with predictive value. When projecting fractal configurations using certain economic barometers such as Stock Indices, it becomes possible to identify turning points and accelerations in a broader range of human endeavor, such as anticipating future political events. This was the focus of the author's timely book: *When* will the Illuminati Crash the Stock Market?

Fractal Analysis can be applied to other types of investment vehicles and is not limited to the financial markets reviewed in this chapter. For example, it has application in forecasting price movements or percentage values in related fields such as real estate, housing starts, and mortgage interest rates.

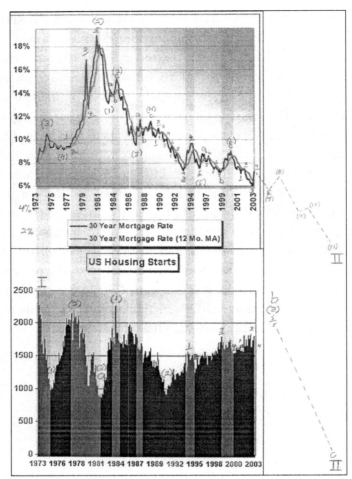

In 2005, the author forecasted the bursting of the Real Estate Bubble that began in 2006 – 2007. The projected dismal future is graphically illustrated.

7

CAPITAL MANAGEMENT

Without a workable money management strategy, an investor gives up some of the advantages that are conferred by Fractal Analysis. Observing the technique discussed in this chapter will provide an added buffer of safety when attempting trade executions. This basic approach can enhance profitability and lessen the chance for incurring losses. Failure to follow these suggested guidelines will increase overall trading risk.

SUBDIVIDING CAPITAL

Give a portion to seven, and also to eight; for thou knowest not what evil shall be upon the earth. – Ecclesiastes 11:2

It is vitally important to be properly capitalized for the kind of trading or investing that one is proposing to undertake.

The total amount of investment capital should be equally divided among markets traded. The author does not recommend simultaneously trading more than two markets. Doing so detracts from the time available for the study of a particular market, and thereby diffuses focus of the comprehensive Analysis.

Capital allocated for a particular market should be divided into 8 subunits of equal amount. Each subunit represents a new purchase of a position – stocks or contracts. (If trading Options, allocate 4 subunits for purchasing Calls, 4 subunits for Puts.) Broker commissions are deducted from the subunit amounts when establishing and exiting a position.

Typically, after up to 4 positions have been established, the new trend will be well underway. At that point, adding further positions may be counterproductive due to the decreasing percentage of the remaining movement. The last 4 units are to be held in reserve should the Analysis prove incorrect. If that situation were to become evident, the other side of the market could be taken with offsetting positions. (For futures trading this would require a second futures brokerage account.) Allocating all 8 units to an open position exposes 100 percent of the capital to potential loss. Unless an analyst is highly skilled in the use of Fractal Analysis, being fully invested is not advised.

Establishing a Position

When an entry point is signaled by the Fractal Analysis, take the first position using one subunit of capital. After making the initial purchase, if another opportunity arises to buy at a lower price (e.g. a small degree fii or fiv correction), a second position should be added, but only if the Analysis is still valid. Likewise, for adding a third and fourth position. Subunits five, six, seven and eight should not be allocated for the same market, or, if trading Options, the same market direction. (Usually, a large percentage of the price movement will have already occurred by the time of the fourth trading opportunity. Any further purchases at higher prices would therefore have a higher attendant risk of sudden reversal.) After establishing the first or subsequent positions, if there is any significant revision to the Fractal Count, or to other trading parameters of the Analysis, the initial position(s) must be reassessed in order to decide if they should be sold, and at what price level most advantageous for liquidation. Assuming the overall Analysis is correct, second, third, and fourth positions should be added at key price retracement levels, thus increasing potential for greater profits at the time of selling. Reducing the average position price by adding more positions at a lower cost at key junctures (Options), or adding slightly higher priced positions during the F1 or F3 stage of the fractal configuration (Stocks, Futures, Forex), when implemented together with a correct Fractal Count, will substantially enhance profitability and lower risk by establishing positions in the direction of the 5 fractal trend. In contrast, if the analyst were to take only one subunit position, with correct Analysis, he would do well. But, if he added more positions, or more positions at a lower cost per position, he would do much better, having incrementally committed further capital at a lower price per share/contract, and when further price data was available at a time the Analysis was more transparent, thus having a higher degree of certainty.

In the case of a favorable trending market, by incrementally adding contracts, an enhanced profitability can be realized. If a trader were to allocate the total sum of *all* 8 units of his capital to the *initial* position, in an adverse move he would be forced to sell and suffer a percentage loss, and could perhaps even incur a total or near total loss of his capital (Options). In making incremental purchases and sustaining a loss, only a fraction of his total capital is affected. If the initial purchase was for only one subunit, a significant loss is not likely to soon occur.

In a confirmed trend, such as one proceeding from F2 to F3, the 4 subunits may be strategically deployed in the manner described above. Long-term stock or futures investors should incrementally commit most of their available capital – or all 8 units of their available capital – to their chosen company or market at key F2 and F4 terminal correction levels. A short-term trader should never commit all his allocated funds to a single market, restricting capital allocation to a maximum of 1/2 the total available funding (4 units). It is never wise to be fully invested for the short-term, even if the Fractal Count warrants committing more funds to an existing position. The window of opportunity may suddenly close after the start of what appeared to be a new five sequence fractal trend, thus quickly losing back profits that were initially gained. Typically, the market price or option premium rapidly increases from the termination of F2 to middle and latter stages of F3, or from F4 to the termination of F5. Therefore, making additional purchases after fii of F3 or fii of F5 will be at a higher cost and with a higher risk of sudden reversal during a fast moving F3 or a shortened or aborted F5.

It is usually best to establish a new position just before the close of the market that is being traded. Making an intra-day entry, or waiting until after the open to make an entry, may result in paying a much higher price, since markets can often gap overnight, and large institutional investors frequently place their orders at the close of the previous day. Also, buying shortly after the initial strong open exposes a late trade to a fii retracement that instantly traps the position on the wrong side of the market. In a fiii of F3 open there will not be an opportunity to buy at a stalled correction since the price will be increasing at its fastest rate. The goal of the analyst is to strive to be positioned *before* the price makes a significant move in the desired direction. A thorough understanding of the fractal analytic approach will make that a realistic objective.

EXITING A POSITION

At a predefined Sell Zone (next chapter), all the shares/contracts should be sold at the same time. When selling for a profit or loss, add the position totals and divide by 8 to determine the next incremental subunit amount.

Simultaneously trading multiple related markets (e.g. stocks), or purchasing option contracts at different Strike Prices in the same market, is not recommended because of incurring further brokerage fees at the time of buying and selling the position, and also because it necessitates an additional step when exiting that requires more time to execute the trade. This last factor becomes important when a position needs to be immediately exited on short notice, such as during an aborted fv of F5 reversal. Any delay in split second timing at the time of selling during a fast moving market can significantly reduce profits.

There are several different types of orders that can be entered when establishing or exiting a position. Some order types have advantages over others. The very worst order is a *Market Order*. This essentially gives the floor broker the liberty of filling an order at the *least* advantageous price recorded during the time interval required to execute the trade. Needless to say, except in unusual circumstances – such as the market about to close – a trader should never enter an order *At the Market*. This gives the Market Maker a *license to steal*. The best order type is a *Limit Order* which instructs the floor broker to fill the trade at a specific price – no higher or lower. Buying or selling a position using a Limit Order insures against price gouging or so-called "slippage." Changing the Limit Order to accommodate Bid/Ask price changes as the market fluctuates is a recommended procedure for capturing additional profits from the price spread, or to quickly exit when the market has reached its full extent and is beginning to reverse.

ORDER EXECUTION

When a buy order has been filled, it immediately must show a loss in the account balance. This is because of the Bid/Ask spread. The lower Bid price is the price at which the Market Maker on the floor of the exchange would like you to liquidate your position when selling. The higher Ask price is the price at which he would like you to pay when establishing a position. The difference between the Bid and Ask price is called the Spread. (This fluctuating amount represents how the Market Maker earns a living.) The Bid price is the price at which the market is quoted. The purchase price when entering or exiting a position is always somewhere between the Bid and Ask spread. Orders to purchase should be entered at or slightly above the lower Bid price, which is the lowest possible fillable price at the time of entering the order. To get a fill, the Market Maker must lower the Bid price in response to the market moving adversely to the order. Therefore, whatever price is entered when buying will immediately register a loss in the trader's brokerage account. Likewise, orders to sell should be at or slightly below the higher Ask price. In this manner, the lowest price is paid at the time of purchase, and the highest price is paid when selling. Having the ability to quickly change the price of an unexecuted order, or to cancel an existing order, will often provide an advantage in a rapid price changing environment. Generally, orders should only be placed at the time of intended market entry or exit as determined by the Fractal Analysis applied to shorter-term charts. Preset buy and sell advance orders are subject to errors in the Analysis that were not discovered in time to cancel or change the purchase order. This could result in significant losses from being on the wrong side of the market.

An Additional Buffer for Safeguarding Capital

The first priority of any trader or analyst is *capital preservation*. The best technician in the world can make one error and lose considerable capital, or even be wiped out in a single trade. Good traders (and especially bad ones) may suffer from the affliction of being *overconfident*. This necessarily follows, since an accomplished market analyst has a long history of successes to his credit and has established proven competence over a meaningful period of time. If human beings were infallible, unwarranted confidence would not be a problem in the world of high risk. But in reality, mistakes do occur, and in this particular endeavor, can be fatal.

In recognition of the realities implicit in trading financial markets, a further strategy should be implemented as a safeguard against overzealous investors and speculators hoping to "break the bank" with their analytical prowess. It is therefore recommended that the analyst/trader not be the same individual who makes the money management decisions. These are separate functions that should rightly be divorced from each other, neither person having knowledge or control over the activities of the other. The analyst, analyzes; the money manager manages the money, determining the unit size and number of units to be allocated. The trader/analyst should be restricted to only one unit of capital at a time. The addition of further units are contingent upon approval by the money manager. (This assumes that the money manager has at least some technical expertise for which to evaluate the trade recommendations of the market analyst.) A total of 4 subunits should be the maximum permitted to be allocated to a series of trade entries. The remaining 4 subunits are always held in reserve. At the time of liquidating subunits 1 through 4, the proceeds are added to the total capital funding (4 reserve subunits + balance of subunits, plus profits or minus losses). Dividing by 8 produces the next subunit size for allocation to the subsequent trading sequence. In this manner, the maximum potential for loss is limited to 50 percent of the total capital stake.

This approach is significantly different from the previous strategy proposed in this chapter, and provides a higher degree of safety by separating two functions which are commonly handled by the same individual. Although this arrangement may reduce ongoing profits, in the longer-term it can substantially increase profitability by preserving capital and increasing the subunit size.

Institutional investors may implement an approach similar to that just described, but the small investor is typically a "one-man show." Unless he is able to summon vast discipline resources as a trader – enduring psychological pressures caused by sudden greed and fear – in this particular arena a potential exists that he may suddenly find himself "unemployed."

8 | SUMMARY: PUTTING IT ALL TOGETHER

Once the Fractal Count has been established and corroborated by the Confirming Indicators and support/resistance levels established by Golden Ratio Arcs and Trendlines, the Moving Average Envelope, Bollinger Bands; and the 18, 50, or 200 bar Simple Moving Averages; the price movement is expected to unfold according to the Fractal Pattern. The following techniques are means to further guide the trade execution process with an even higher degree of precision, defining both the time and narrow price range in which to make a buy or sell decision.

RULE OF 3: DIRECTIONAL ARROWS

As a quick and convenient visual guide for targeting tradable turning points, the author has devised a helpful system to further identify the terminal reversal range of a 5 or 3 fractal pattern. In recognizing that the 3rd and 5th fractals (or in a continuation trend, the 7th and 9th, or 11th and 13th, etc.) are the last two upward (advancing market) or downward (declining market) price bar movements, and that the price direction will subsequently reverse on the next (third) price bar, it is therefore convenient to label these terminal price bars using two arrows in the primary direction, followed by one reversed arrow in the opposing direction. The second arrow indicates when to sell (S), or Buy (B). Likewise for the 1st and 3rd fractal price bars in a correction. The following illustrates this concept.

Advancing Market:

	S	
↑	↑	↓
F3	F5	F1

Declining Market:

↓	↓	↑
F3	F5	F1
	B	

"NO TRADE"

There are times when the Analysis is inconclusive, when the Fractal Count could be interpreted to yield at least two possible outcomes for the next bar or series of bars. In these instances, a "No Trade" designation (NT) should label the second Directional Arrow in order to alert the analyst not to take a position at the next potential opportunity. Over-trading, or being too eager to enter the next trade, increases risk if the level of trade certainty is not heavily weighted in favor of the Analysis being correct.

Advancing Market:

	NT	
↑	↑	↓
F3	F5	F1

Declining Market:

↓	↓	↑
F3	F5	F1
	NT	

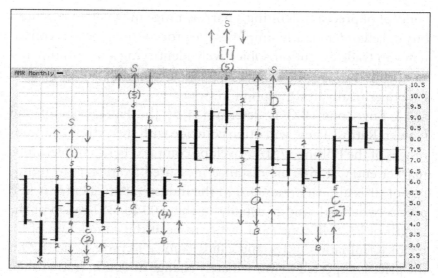

Directional arrows applied to a correct Fractal Count.

BUY, SELL, AND REVERSE ZONES

Deciding when to precisely enter and exit a position can sometimes seem arbitrary, even with the advantage of a correct Fractal Count supported by select Confirming Indicators and levels of support/resistance. Traders are known to "freeze" at that crucial decision juncture, either waiting too long to make the purchase, and thus missing the lowest price; or prematurely making an entry that yet has more adverse price movement or Option contract time depreciation. In either case, at a critical point the trader/investor did not make the best use of the Analysis, and with consequent opportunity loss.

Much of the angst associated with buy/sell decisions is eliminated by developing a high degree of proficiency with the comprehensive Fractal Analysis methodology. Yet, there are certain psychological barriers that need to be overcome before the advantages conferred by the study can be applied without fear and trepidation. Even seasoned traders require further psychological detachment in order to distance themselves from the emotional pressure of committing funds to a new position. Addressing this issue, the concept of precisely defining a narrow range in which to execute a buy or sell order greatly simplifies the process and provides consistency in trade execution. Objectively identifying a maximum and minimum range *in advance* allows for eliminating later subjectivity at a critically decisive point in time.

A Buy Zone (BZ) is determined by the Fractal Count and Golden Ratios. These will often coincide with the extreme or mid-ranges of the Bollinger/MA Envelope complex. For example, an F2 market entry at .618 the distance measured from start to terminus of F1 is almost a standard in the industry. An F4 entry is also precisely defined, and is usually in the .500 to .382 range of the length of F3. Sell Zone (SZ) exits can be at the completion of F1, F3, or termination of F5; and can become a Reverse Zone (RZ) if the price is expected to immediately change direction (rather than form a continuation trend, or make a long corrective F2 retracement after the initial F1 reversal). A trader's life would be greatly simplified if the Golden Ratios were all that was needed for making buy and sell order entry decisions. However, in the real world of market manipulation, where everyone knows these ratios exist and their exact location in any given market, something more is needed for the successful trader to anticipate sudden reversals and aborted targets. Therefore, the concept of "Zones" was devised by the author to provide a clearly predefined range at which to enter and exit a position. The trade decision point does not have to be any specific price or calculated ratio, but is a narrow price area encompassing the most likely turning points based on the overall Analysis. An order is entered somewhere within the range of the BZ or SZ and is automatically executed whenever the market price enters that range. (But the trade is not entered until the price reaches the specified zone.) Buy/Sell orders are triggered without having to adjust for minute changes in the price of the underlying market. (For options, Bid/Ask premiums can also be used to establish an entry/exit range.)

Identifying a narrow zone where the price will reach a terminal phase before reversing provides a distinct advantage. Locate this band width on the price chart being traded, for example, the Daily chart. As long as the Analysis is still proving correct at the time of purchasing or selling, enter a buy or sell order set to execute within this range. (For Futures, move the BZ/SZ such that the price will *penetrate* the zone and the trade order will fill.)

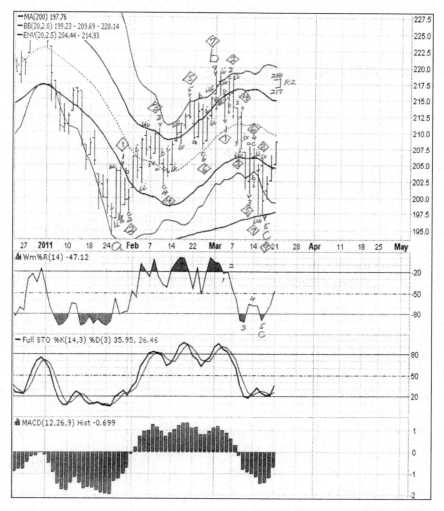

Precision Buy, Sell, and Reverse Zones can be determined in advance. This chart is a continuation of a previous chart (chapter 2) illustrating the Alternating Principle and showing a Diamond Count clarification. Note that F2 of C corrected nearly 100% of F1; fii of F3 of C corrected *more than* 100% of fi. Alternating Principle was subsequently evident for *aborted* fiv of F3 and comparative *very long* fiv of F5.

Additional confirmation of buy and sell areas can be obtained by Golden Ratio Arcs and Trendlines for the time interval traded, and also from longer-term charts. Without this visual BZ/SZ guide, a profitable trade can quickly turn into a losing position, or no trade at all because of a missed opportunity to establish a position.

PRICE MOMENTUM VERSUS SPEED

Fast decline, price breaks through support

Momentum is the persistent force driving a market in either direction. The speed at which this occurs is dependent upon several factors relative to the Fractal Count. For example, F3 tends to move at a greater rate of speed than does corrective F4, which requires proportionally more time to completion; F2 is often sharply counter to F1 and reverses much of the F1 initial movement when rapidly changing trend direction. In either case, the momentum is established in the new direction but the speed is a variable. Throughout the fractal 5 - 3 configuration pattern, the price direction and momentum shift at irregular intervals, and so does the speed.

The velocity at which the price is moving will affect the resistance or "friction" inhibiting that price movement. Greater speed of price movement will break through support or resistance levels that would have otherwise reversed a slower-moving pattern.

Slow decline, support holds, price advances

Stand back from the internal analysis (Fractal Count, Confirming Indicators, Price Channels, Moving Averages) to decide what the Speed vs. Momentum is telling you. Often, it is giving a loud and clear signal. Typically, during a strong and persistent price advance, there are fast reversals off corrective lows and slow reversals off terminal tops. Conversely, during a price decline there are fast reversals off corrective highs and slow reversals off lows.

MISSING AND PHANTOM FRACTALS

Sometimes in a fast or extended movement the last subunit of the 5 or 3 fractal sequence is omitted or shortened to such an extent that it is not fully formed and appears to be "missing." (In special instances it truly *is* missing and simply did not materialize.) While this does not occur very often in the larger degree intervals (Quarterly - Yearly), it can be seen more frequently on the smaller degree time frames (1 Minute - Hourly). In being aware of this potential, the analyst is better able to interpret price action at key turning points, and thus exit a position before completion of an extended F5 or FC, where a missing terminal subunit is most likely to occur. An example of a missing fractal is seen in the previous Directional Arrow chart: F5 of FC of [2].

In order to justify your Count you may sometimes "imagine" a subunit fractal is evident when in reality it does not exist. Such experimenter bias happens quite often in the world of scientific investigation, and is by no means uncommon when money is involved and there is an incentive to prove your analysis correct, even though it is not. As a general rule: "If you don't see it, don't label it." Phantom fractals have a way of appearing when the stakes are high and you cannot afford to be wrong.

At the other end of the spectrum, don't make the mistake of assuming the present count is "too easy" and therefore "everyone else knows it." Typically, everyone else *does not* know it. Just one glance at the Put/Call ratios will tell you there are usually an approximately equal number of contracts or shares on either side of most markets nearly all of the time. So one side is always wrong and the other side either knows what they are doing or simply guessed right. (For most traders and investors in the financial and commodity markets, taking on positions is like betting on the horses or playing Roulette at a casino; they haven't got a clue what the market will do next, only a *hunch* what it *might* do. But that and a couple of bucks will buy you a tee shirt.) Conversely, avoid thinking the Count is too difficult and cannot be correctly known; don't make the Analysis any more difficult than it actually is.

VIEWING MULTIPLE TIME FRAME CHARTS

In today's fast moving market environment, where insider trading and preset triggered computerized buy and sell programs can create exaggerated price fluctuations in a matter of seconds, maintaining one's objectivity of a short-term time frame can be facilitated by referencing the next longer time interval chart. For example, if trading the Daily chart, a context perspective is achieved by comparing the current series of Daily price bars to the single price bar on the Weekly chart. In this way, an inexplicable bar registering on the Daily chart can be accounted for by referencing the Weekly, or even the Monthly chart.

If short-term trading – opening and closing positions during the same day – direct more of your analysis on the Hourly and 30 Minute charts, and not so much on 15 Minute - 1 Minute charts. If swing trading within the 1 to 3 Week time frame interval, ignore the 1 Minute - 30 Minute chart action and fix your gaze on the Daily and Hourly charts. The Fractal Count and Confirming Indicators – especially the MACD Histogram and Stochastic – should be the focus of your attention. Broadening the scope of the time interval charts being observed will prevent you from making knee-jerk reactions to buy and sell based on irrelevant price swings, some of which are *intended* to "shake out" positions in potentially profitable trades. When the Fractal Analysis indicates a buy or sell, *then* look at smaller time interval charts to precision time your entry or exit.

The advantage of maintaining all the charts recommended by the Fractal Analysis is a matter of *perspective*. This is one of the major failures of computer-generated software: the ability to integrate seemingly divergent data from multiple chart views into a meaningful and cohesive whole. This propensity is unique to the human mind. Moving from one time frame chart to the next allows for more or less detail to be revealed and collated. Switching to a larger time frame simplifies and clarifies interpretation of fractal patterns seen on smaller scale intervals. Without the perspective of the next longer-term chart, the price data loses a point of reference and could have multiple interpretations. The advantage gained by viewing longer or shorter time frames is one of the reasons why the author's Fractal Analysis is so consistently accurate.

Computer programs generating quantitative price labels according to a rigid set of parameters are infamous for frequently changing the count analysis. In the final consideration, there is *only one* Fractal Count, and it *is* determinable in advance.

Keep your eye on the longer-term charts!

WHAT TO DO WHEN IT GOES AGAINST YOU

You established a position based on your best understanding of Fractal Analysis; you had what you believed was a correct Fractal Count. The Confirming Indicators and support/resistance levels all showed that a market entry was warranted at the specified BZ calculated from these support/resistance levels, the Golden Ratio, and Alternating Principle. You did everything right, or so you thought. But ... your analysis was *wrong*. And now the market is moving against you and your account is losing money. What do you do?

First of all, don't sell until you can find your mistake and identify where the price is currently located within the fractal configuration on all time frames. Then, and only then, make a decision to either wait for a more opportune time to exit, buy more, or hold. Sometimes you will generate the most profit by simply doing nothing.

Making a quick reassessment of the Analysis requires having developed a practiced facility for working with the fractal concept. A beginner cannot do this. You must be skilled, or do not attempt to trade until having acquired the necessary expertise to rapidly assess a situation and decide the most advantageous course in which to proceed. Sudden rash decisions are much more likely to result in losses than an objective examination of the facts.

If you followed the Capital Management strategy presented in this book when taking your first or second position, the worst possible outcome will not significantly affect your total account funding. This is a fail-safe feature built into the comprehensive Fractal Analysis that will serve to minimize the potential for losses should you become positioned on the wrong side of a market. But even then, a short-term loss can be turned into a gain if the market will soon reverse direction, or if taking the other side of an established position to offset accruing losses. An impulsive reaction to "sell everything" is seldom the best course of action to take, and should only be considered once the price location has been definitively identified in all the time interval charts and it has been determined that the price will not recover. For example, if a position was established on the short side of a market at the termination of fii of an F3 of (F3) advance, there exists a high probability that a substantial permanent loss will be incurred for the funds allocated to that position. In this case, the most effective course would be to establish a counter offsetting long position to capture the expected sudden rise in price, and simultaneously liquidate the short position. Failure to do so would most likely result in an unrecoverable loss.

When the market is moving against you, remain calm and study the situation before making a decision on whether to take action or do nothing. There is almost always a better price to get out of a market. Sudden spikes – either up or down – tend to be followed by a movement in the opposite direction, the extent of which can be calculated by one of the Golden Ratio derivatives: .618, .500, .382, .236. Establishing an offsetting position, and holding both positions during a short-term correction, will often salvage what could have been a significant loss.

When things are "going badly," your focus should not be the price action showing on your computer screen, but instead the hard copy of your various time interval charts which you have attached to separate clipboards. Starting with the Yearly or Quarterly chart, work your way backward until you arrive at the time interval being traded. Carefully study your Analysis applied to the Yearly, Quarterly, Monthly, Weekly, Daily charts to see if you can discover your mistake. Chances are you mislabeled something – an F3 that you thought was F5; an FC of an F4 correction that was actually FA (a common mistake). When you finally discern where the price is located on the time frame you are trading, *then* look at your screen to break it into even smaller intervals: Hourly, 30 Minutes, 15 Minutes, etc. Until that point, keep your head down and concentrate on the paper charts, otherwise, all you will do is cause yourself unnecessary anxiety that will further cloud your judgment. When the "ah-ha" moment suddenly comes into view, at least you will know where the price is located, and can then take action based on a clearer and better understanding. Sometimes it helps to simply turn off the computer and walk away, do something else, forget the market for a while. You know what it's going to do, right? So why aggravate yourself worrying about it? Tomorrow will be different; everything will change – in your favor. The *correct* Analysis says so.

Becoming an effective and successful market analyst is a process; it does not occur overnight. On the day you can confidently stand in the face of danger and adversity, you will know that you have *arrived*. And may God Almighty be with you!

FRACTAL ANALYSIS OF THE U.S. STOCK MARKET

The importance of building a price/time framework has been stressed throughout this book. This defining structure serves as a confirming guide to project future price movements as determined by the Fractal Count. A true count of the fractal subunits will tend to coincide with the framework, and thus provide a self-correcting future price configuration.

Using the Dow Jones Industrial Average as an example, the key to analyzing this particular market is in recognizing the terminal point of highest degree in a long-term price history that can only be ascertained with certainty by tracing this market back to the inception of the NYSE in 1792. Identifying 1978 as the completion of Fractal [4], it then becomes a matter of labeling each yearly price bar relative to larger and smaller degrees that culminated in the long-term ⑦ top in 2007. In the two subsequent years, a 3 fractal breakdown developed until 2009, which found support at the Golden Ratio 1.618 level. It was important to recognize the 2007-2009 decline as a 3 fractal movement, rather than a 5 fractal advance, as will later be seen in comparisons using the Alternating Principle. The Quarterly chart shown below proves by means of a Diamond Count that this decline consisted of a 3 fractal movement which formed a 7 or 11 continuation.

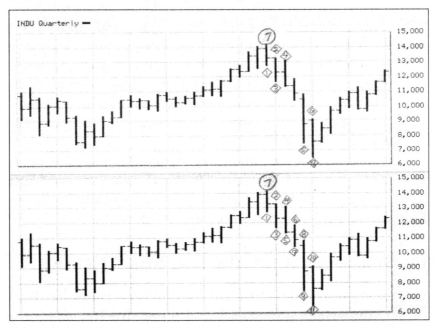

Referencing the Yearly chart to follow, notice how the Golden Ratio Trendlines act as both support and resistance during the ensuing advance to ⑨, which completes terminal [F5]. From the ⑧ 2009 DJIA low at approximately 6500, any further advance would be expected to encounter resistance starting at 11,500 in 2010, then at 12,500 in 2011, 13,500 in 2012, 14,500 or 16,500 in 2013, 17,500 in 2014, and 18,000 in 2015.

After the projected market advance terminus in 2015, support and resistance Golden Ratio Trendlines provide the framework for the [FA] - [FB] - [FC] 5 year decline until the year 2020.

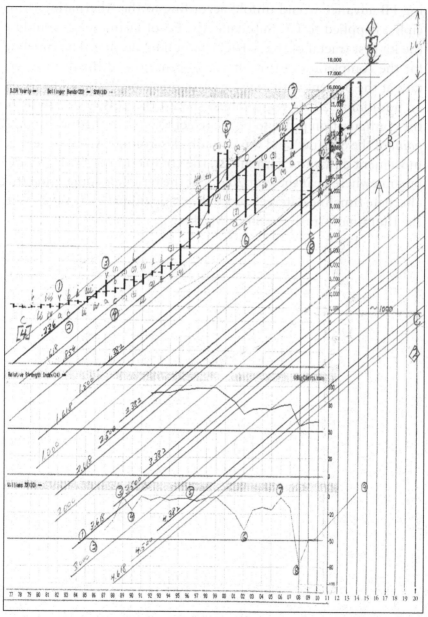

Yearly Projected Future of Dow Jones Industrial Average 1978 – 2020

The possibility exists that FC of Diamond 2 could become FA. In that case, the decline level would not be as shown in the chart but would find support at a higher price. The structure of an ensuing FB advance would unfold according to the Alternating Principle as applied to FA. Subsequently, FC of Diamond 2 would be the longest fractal of the A-B-C Diamond 2 decline. The timeline for the completion of this alternate scenario is difficult to ascertain at the present with any degree of precision, but could require an additional 20-30 years. Thus, should the author's analysis of the configuration prove to be incorrect for specifying the *terminal point* of the decline, (and was actually describing FA, not the entire movement down to Diamond 2), the completion of FB-FC would be somewhere near the year 2051. For the rationale supporting this alternate timeline date, reference the companion book: *When* Will the Illuminati Crash the Stock Market?

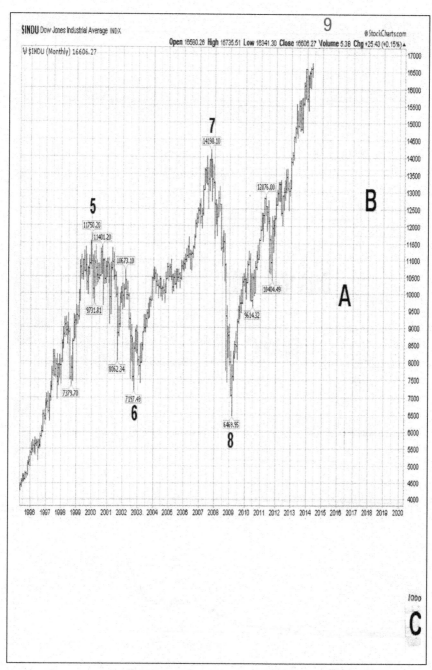

Monthly Projected Future of Dow Jones Industrial Average 1995 – 2020

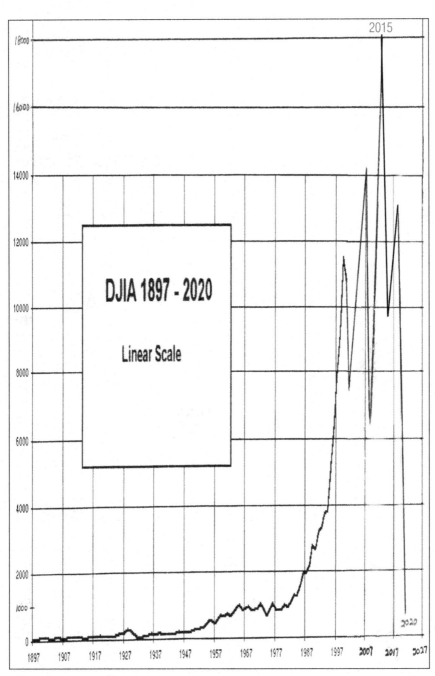

Yearly Projected Future of Dow Jones Industrial Average 1897 – 2020

EXAMPLE OF A FRACTAL TRADE

You have annotated multiple time frame charts with a Fractal Count. You have observed the Money Management Strategy by subdividing your capital into 8 equal subunits. You grasp the significance of the 4 key confirming Momentum Indicators, the price Channels and Moving Averages, in relation to the current price direction and momentum. Further, you have identified in advance a Buy Zone entry range and Sell Zone exit range based upon these objective criteria. You are familiar with the market you are trading, having paper traded it for at least 3-6 months, and believe that you are now prepared to make your first purchase using 1 subunit of capital and buying at least 4 months of time value on the option contract. (This example can also apply to Stock, Futures, and Forex purchases.) After a final check of the Fractal Count on minor degree time frame charts - 2 Hour, 1 Hour, 30 Minutes, 15 minutes, 5 minutes - a half hour before the market close you plan to enter an Online order to open a position. You will buy At-The-Money or nearest Out-Of-The-Money Call or Put options; as many contracts as your 1 subunit amount allows. The 7 units of remaining capital remain in cash reserve, uncommitted to a market position.

You have transferred the Fractal Count from the Monthly to the Weekly to the Daily chart, and will be taking the trade signals from the Daily Chart. You also have the same Count for the smaller degree time frame charts and can therefore see in advance the upcoming terminal point of the current price action. On the Daily chart you add 3 directional arrows to show 2 arrows in the direction of the current trend, and 1 arrow reversing to the opposite direction. You will buy on the second arrow, near the close of the market.

The Monthly chart below shows the Fractal Analysis as described in this book. Additional annotations could be added, such as Golden Ratio Arcs and Trendlines. This chart may have required a longer-term chart, such as Quarterly or Yearly, in order to gain perspective for deriving the terminal endpoint marked with a large red "X". Referring to a chart of larger degree than the trading time frame chart (Weekly, Daily, Hourly) provides a confirming context for establishing a reliable Count that can then be transferred to smaller trading time frame charts.

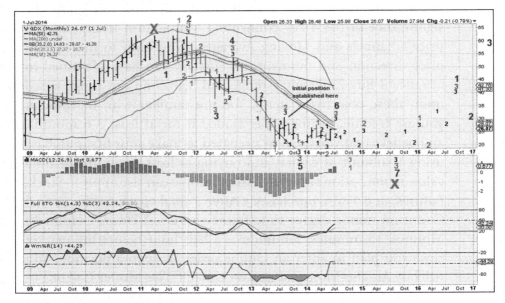

After 5 minutes, your initial order for Buying to Open did not execute at the "Bid" price that you selected. With 20 minutes remaining until the market close, you change your order to between the Bid and Ask price. Five minutes later it still did not execute. Now, with 15 minutes remaining, you change the order again to the Ask price and it immediately executes. You have bought 5 Nearest Strike Price Put Option Contracts, with 4 months of time value, for a price of $275 each. Total cost to establish this position was $1395, including broker commission.

You took a position at what you thought was the termination of a corrective Fractal 2 in an established downtrend of a three phase decline, but five days later the market is moving contrary to your position and you are losing money. What should you do?

First, check the Fractal Counts and Confirming Indicators for the smaller time frames and for the trading time frame. If the trade still has upside resistance and downside potential, hold to observe the short-term momentum and to confirm a holding position. The next day it moves against you once more, but the upside momentum is weak. You hold for a third day and it advances again, but only at the open and for the first hour. You notice it penetrated significant support levels on the 2 Hour, 1 Hour, and 30 minute charts, so you make a second purchase, at a lower price, for the same total amount as before. You now have 10 more contracts, for a total of 15, and cumulative cost of $2740. The market closes substantially down off its opening high, and your position is now showing a slight profit.

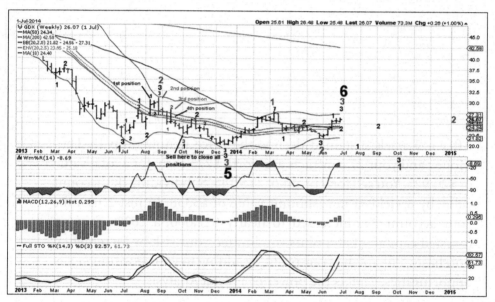

Following a subsequent 3 week decline, and more profits, it suddenly reverses on the fourth week. You hold once again, your account having lost most of its gain. You notice the Daily price stopped at the top of the declining MA Envelope, and the Daily momentum Indicators are down or reversing. You make a third purchase for the same dollar amount, adding 8 more contracts for a total of 23, and a cumulative cost of $4175. On the next day it reverses downward and closes the week at the bottom of its range.

You make a fourth and final purchase, adding 4 more contracts totaling 27, for a cumulative cost of $5,780.

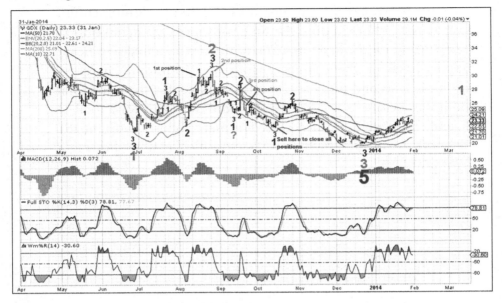

After a 3 week sustained decline the price is now deep In-The-Money and your 27 contracts are worth $775 each, for a total value of $20,925. You sell for a profit of $15,145. Subdividing the account value by 8 yields a new subunit value of $3338. In just 2 months your account has increased to nearly $27,000, a 262% gain on invested capital. At all points you limited your risk by incremental purchases, enhancing your profit by adding to your position at key opportunities. *That* is the power of Fractal Analysis!

APPENDICES

Quick Reference Guide for Risk Management

Trading Risk Increases When:

1. Wrong Fractal Count.
2. All or most of the capital is committed to a single market position.
3. Not buying in subunit increments.
4. Poor entry from not establishing a precision Buy Zone.
5. Not first checking the trade with the Confirming Indicators.
6. Not applying a Fractal Count to Confirming Indicators.
7. Not applying the Alternating Principle.
8. Ignoring upper support/resistance levels.
9. Misreading or ignoring correspondence between price and price range bands, MA Envelopes and key Moving Averages, and momentum indicators.
10. Failing to correlate trading time frame chart to longer/shorter-term charts.
11. Purchasing too little time (applies to trading options).
12. Failing to follow or act on your Analysis.

SOME KEY POINTS OF FRACTAL TRADING

1. Fractal Counts for all time frames must be in agreement.

2. Identify application of Alternating Principle. For short-term trading: Weekly and Daily charts. For longer-term hold strategy: Yearly, Quarterly, Monthly charts.

3. Expected price direction should not be in conflict with *longer-term* Confirming Indicators.

4. For the time frame being traded, observe where the price is located in relation to Bollinger Bands; MA Envelope; 18, 50, 200 bar Moving Average support/resistance levels. On the next longer time interval charts, note the trading ranges between Bollinger Bands and Moving Average Envelopes; and between the 3 Moving Averages verses Bollinger Bands and MA Envelopes.

5. Notice where the 3 momentum Confirming Indicators are located in relation to their midlines and extremes of oscillator range.

6. Calculate Golden Ratios to gauge retracement levels.

7. Always show Buy Zones, Sell Zones, Reverse Zones in terms of a specific narrow range determined by Golden Ratios, the Fractal Count, and the price volatility support/resistance framework (BB, MA Envelope, MA's).

8. Check all time frame charts carefully; examine small details relative to Confirming Indicators and BB/MA channels vs. Moving Average crossings.

9. Give greater consideration to longer-term trading time frames: (Weekly > Daily > Hourly > 30 Minute > 15 Minute > 5 Minute > 1 Minute)

10. Do not chase the price when buying or selling. Know where the price is going and hold until it hits your specified price range target.

11. Make additional purchases whenever the market temporarily moves contrary to the expected direction without invalidating the Analysis.

12. Use Directional Arrows to indicate 3, 5, and start of 1 trend change.

13. A correct Fractal Count takes precedence over momentum Confirming Indicators and support/resistance levels.

14. Successful traders have a *disciplined* approach. They do not establish or exit positions based on emotional reactions or unsupported assumptions. Maintain your objectivity at all times.

C FRACTALS
COUNTING IN 3's

The typical 5 - 3 fractal configuration can be altered to a 3 - 3 configuration, depending upon the market, prevailing market conditions, and perhaps even intentional subterfuge on the part of industry insiders to confuse those implementing a counting strategy based on a 5 - 3 predefined criterion. While this changeable count is not typical, the astute analyst should be aware that it is possible and can occur. Failure to recognize a change from the expected pattern will result in out of phase timing that either holds a position for too long a duration or gives false signals for entry into a market at inopportune junctures, such as when reaching an unexpected major terminal point of reversal. The following shows a 3 fractal count. Observe that all the rules of fractal counting still apply, but there are no small degree fiv's and fv's in the trending direction. Notice the Alternating Principle in effect for the subunits comprising F1, F3, F5 of F(1). This atypical count can only be ascertained in advance by referencing the longer-term charts.

The reader is left to complete the 3 - 3 fractal structure as an exercise.

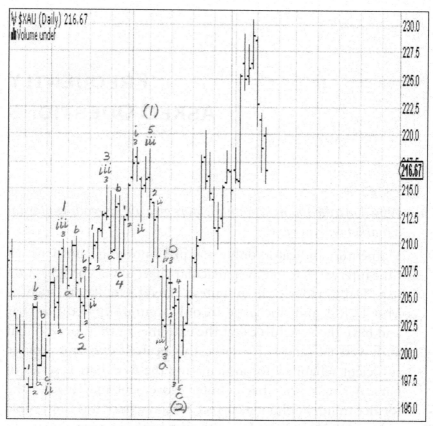

Daily chart showing an atypical 3 Fractal Count

FREQUENTLY ASKED QUESTIONS

1) *Why don't the momentum indicators give a true reading of what a market will do next?*

   Momentum Indicators only gauge price movement until the last time interval (bar) on the particular chart under consideration (e.g. Daily, Hourly, 15 minutes). Trend Oscillators such as MACD, RSI, and Stochastic are only accurate up to the last bar and have their usefulness at the extremes of their overbought and oversold ranges. However, this in itself does not provide sufficient reliability for anticipating the next bar or series of bars. A single price bar counter movement may reverse the former trend. Without a correct Fractal Count it is impossible to know the next price bar with any degree of certainty.

2) *How many markets should I trade? Is it better to trade more than one market?*

   The author does not recommend trading more than two markets. An analyst's time and focus should be on a single market, and at most two, not diffused over a range of different markets or separate stock issues. (90 percent of all stocks can be classified as 1 market.) Another market can be considered as part of the overall Analysis used to confirm the primary market under study, but should be either a complimentary or contrary trending market that will provide additional confirmation for the primary market being traded. For example, the Bond market generally moves contrary to the Stock Indices.

3) *Why does the Fractal Count seem to change as the price movement develops?*

The Fractal pattern is only static in retrospect. As to whether or not it existed before the price is recorded is a topic for discussion and debate. This author contends that it *does* exist in a predetermined form, but that form can be slightly modified or warped to the extreme in response to market reactions to outside factors or events. For example, sudden freezing cold weather in Florida can instantly reverse the futures Orange Juice market and abort an F5 decline. The factors preceding an economic collapse are clearly reflected in advance by the price movement and behavior of large Stock Indices such as the DJIA.

A so-called "changed" Fractal Count assumes one's initial analysis was correct, which is not always the case. Especially for the novice trader, typically, the Count is wrong on at least one time frame chart. It is only by familiarity with the basic fractal concept and comprehensive Analysis, that with repeated exposure to a particular market, a true graphic picture emerges. In hindsight, the analyst learns from his past mistakes and is subsequently better equipped when encountering a similar Fractal Count in the future.

4) *Determining the Fractal Count seems like a laborious process. Why can't I just buy software that automatically assigns numerical designations and retracement levels?*

While software providers are hoping you will purchase their products, a computer-generated annotation is only as accurate as the program algorithm from which it operates. The complexity of the human brain is yet superior to any computerized virtual assessment of market price behavior. No computer software has the capability of integrating all the time frames into a single coherent scenario, projected into the future, utilizing the Alternating Principle, and identifying when a 5 - 3 fractal configuration will continue to 9 - 7, 13 - 11, 17 - 15, or larger structure. (And no computerized analysis will ever be able to differentiate an atypical 3 - 3 trending market from a 5 - 3.) Omitting these key elements of the Fractal Analysis leaves any computer-generated annotation without referencing vital information that must be taken into consideration in order to yield a price numerical assignment that confers any predictive advantage. Computerized technical analysis is therefore likely to produce a false count. Any software is inadequate for duplicating the brain's flexibility and creativity. Even the most advanced computers can only perform simple deductive tasks when compared to the intellect God can express in a human mind.

5) *Are there any markets that I should avoid? Which are the best markets for trading short-term? Investing long-term?*

Relatively few markets are suitable for trading short-term. Any market that does not fulfill the criterion of having sufficiently large Open Interest should be immediately eliminated from consideration. This would include most of the agricultural and financial futures markets. Likewise, small capitalization stocks. Generally, the larger the market, the less likelihood for experiencing the effects of insider trading and other market manipulations that create sudden price volatility. Long-term investors should also heed these rules, and must be able to "Short" the market should their Analysis forecast significant downside potential. Without implementing a shorting strategy, a "buy and hold" investor runs the same risk as a shorter-term trader.

For both long-term investing and short-term trading, the best tradable markets are the Indexes, which are a representative sample of stocks comprising an industry sector. These tend to be large Open Interest markets (NASDAQ trades over 1 billion shares per day) and therefore have the liquidity to provide a more balanced interplay between buyers and sellers.

6) *Is Day Trading a safe time frame to trade? What is the best trading time frame?*

Timing a market using the shortest time intervals (1 minute, 5 minute, 10 minute, etc) is perhaps the most dangerous approach to maximizing returns. A trader's ability to react to sudden changes in price direction is limited by the speed at which a market can reverse. For this reason it is possible to suffer massive losses in a single day, and perhaps even total loss of one's capital resulting from a price spike reversal that gave too little notice of a changing trend on small interval charts. Automatic "stop losses" can be violated, and frequently are, in response to price manipulation on the part of the Market Makers on the floor of the exchange traded markets. There are too many potentially adverse factors involved in trading the very short-term time interval which makes this a poor choice for anyone hoping to accrue long-term profits. Often, Day Traders seeking to open and close positions during the same trading day lose their capital funding within a brief period of time.

A far better choice of time frame to trade is what is known as "Swing Trading." This is an interval lasting approximately 1 to 3 weeks, and provides a more favorable window of opportunity for executing buy and sell decisions. The analyst is not constantly in a frantic rush to open and close trades, as he is with Day Trading, but has a much longer time frame in which to establish and close out positions. This advantage results in making better trading decisions based on the full compliment of tools and concepts making up Fractal Analysis.

7) *Are Commodity Futures and Index Options "fair markets"?*

In the author's opinion, Commodity Futures markets are implicitly unfair and put the investor at a distinct disadvantage because of the very nature of the markets themselves. Traders hoping to provide protection against counter price movements commonly experience their stop orders being triggered, and often at a loss. (In the futures markets, stop orders exist to be set off. This produces a quick no risk profit for those on the trading floor benefiting from such organized thievery.) It is the author's experience that this occurrence is not a coincidence, but is a function of price manipulation by those individuals on the exchange floor with the authority to arbitrarily adjust prices in direct response to investor positions indicated on their computer monitors. If there is any protection from such criminal activity it is for the futures investor not to use stops, but instead have a large cash margin reserve to draw upon that would greatly lessen the potential for a broker Margin Call demanding to cover a losing position. Margin Calls are standard modus operandi for the Futures brokerage industry: the broker unilaterally commandeering a client's account by issuing *sudden ultimatums* for the trader to deposit additional funds into an account, or else the broker will sell positions to cover the deficit. Unless the investor wishes to acquire an unwanted "rogue trading partner," the author strongly advises against trading Futures. Only those with a minimum of 5 years trading experience and cash reserve funding in a brokerage account equal to at least five times the value of open positions should trade or invest in the Futures markets.

In contrast, Options Trading eliminates many of the negative aspects associated with Commodity Futures. There is no possibility for a broker "Margin Call" because there is no margin required (funds borrowed from the broker) since all settlements are in cash. Like Futures, buying Options on select Indices requires only a fraction of the true value of the purchased asset. While price manipulations on the various Options exchanges do indeed occur – *For the love of money is the root of all evil* (1 Timothy 6:10) – the consequences for the trader are not necessarily detrimental, as in Futures, since a temporary counter price movement will only register a *paper loss* for Options, not a *realized loss* as would speculating with an under-margined Futures account. Further, trading Options on certain Index exchanges requires less capital than trading

Stocks, Futures, or Forex. For all these reasons, Options trading, while not eliminating the issue of price manipulation, provides a trading environment with an attendant greater potential for realizing significant gains.

8) *How much investment capital do I need for trading?*

Capital requirements vary depending upon the chosen investment vehicle and an individual's objectives. For successfully trading Stocks, Futures or the Forex currency markets, a six figure account provides greater protection against adverse price movements and will allow for implementation of a money management strategy that would not be possible with lesser capital amounts. Trading Options can be successfully negotiated starting with only a few hundred dollars (ref. Appendix D). The leveraging factor in Futures, Forex and Options is often 10 to 1, and can be much greater, but only Options has the advantage of controlled downside risk and can be implemented using a fraction of the capital required by other types of trading vehicles. Aways buy at least 4 months of time value.

9) *What do you see as the future for the U.S. economy? What about for Gold and Silver?*

A detailed discussion of the near, intermediate, and long-term future of the U.S. and global economies is presented in the author's book: *When* Will the Illuminati Crash the Stock Market? A Yearly and Monthly projected price chart of the Dow Jones Industrial Average was included in Chapter 8 of this volume. As previously noted, there exists some potential for the projected terminal bottom in 2020 to actually be the first movement [FA] of the expected [A][B][C] decline. If that were the case, the terminus of the global financial meltdown would not occur until approximately the year 2051.

The commodity Spot Gold and Silver markets should move contrary to the Stock Indices. (Since its 2001 low, Gold is counting as 3 fractals, not 5.) Confirming my November 2011 documented forecast, my Fractal Analysis proved correct in identifying the key turning point in the Gold market in the month of September 2011. A top in Silver preceded the Gold terminus by 5 months.

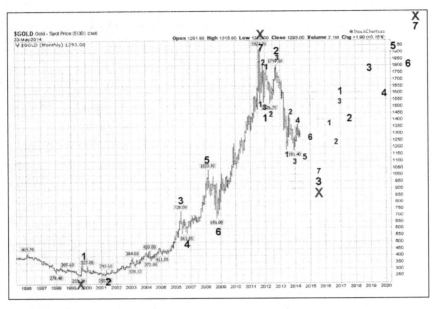

10) *Why don't you use economic news and financial reports to make your analysis?*

News, financial reports, expert opinion polls, and other forms of market-related information are typically biased and predicated on subjective criterion, having little or nothing to do with the technical picture as revealed by the author's Fractal Analysis. Although fundamental information can sometimes be helpful in determining future market price trends and direction (e.g. OPEC announcing an oil trade embargo), it is more often conflicting or has no significant impact on the undercurrent actually moving the markets behind the headlines. The newspaper article below is a case in point: the DJIA advancing in a corrective mode from its first major drop in 2008, en route to a sustained long-term decline. This false recovery, fueled by government intervention "Quantitative Easing" and heavily promoted by the controlled media, is seen by the public as a sign of an economic recovery. However, Illuminati-controlled print publications such as the Cleveland Plain Dealer have another agenda, and that is to seduce and mesmerize the sleeping masses into an even deeper trance state of false security in order to lead them to their own destruction when the elite globalists suddenly "pull the plug" on Wall Street and crash the global economy. (The newspapers print what they *are told* they can print. Staff reporters cannot reveal the facts if those facts are detrimental to the globalist's objectives – e.g. the worldwide aerosol human depopulation spray operation known as *Chemtrails.*) As was true for all dictatorial governments throughout modern history, the media is controlled by a federal government that is controlled by big business corporations. International banking interests own and control the corporations. The banking institutions are owned and controlled by key Illuminati crime families, most prominent of which are the European Rothschilds, who control all the major news outlets in America and throughout the modern Western world. Therefore, any political or economic "news" reported on the main television broadcasting networks is actually *political propaganda* to further the despotic agenda of the world's financial elite. A rule of thumb is to believe *the exact opposite* of what is being reported. *That* will be closer to the truth.

Media disinformation is often what *apparently* drives advancing markets.

11) *From what other people are saying in the news and on the Internet, I get the impression that the stock market could crash any day now. But they've been saying that for years. How can you be so sure the market will crash in 2018 - 2020?*

I agree that financial prognosticators are frequently wrong about their timeline expectations, since most of them are offering an "educated guess" and are not implementing the type of detailed Analysis that I have put forth in two of my books. Additionally, my track record speaks for itself. The technical reasons why I do not believe the market will crash until after 2015 are covered in this book, and the fundamental reasons – based on the Holy Bible – are discussed in the companion volume: *When* Will the Illuminati Crash the Stock Market? Both of these analyses are in perfect timeline agreement. Yet, these dates are subject to minor revision, within the Biblical context, due to the power elite's manipulation of global financial markets in an effort to create more time to make ready their worldwide political/economic system. Should I detect any significant alteration of this expected timeline, and the year 2015 proves not to be precisely accurate for the market top – but only a near approximation for initiating the first of two Crashes (2016-2017; 2018-2020) – I will immediately issue a retraction and a revised updated timeline.

Further, I have previously recognized that the world's financial elite, being very much aware of my publicized forecasting achievements, have responded to advance documented forecasts by a massive cash influx into the stock market at critical fractal turning points in an attempt to prevent a sudden decline. The Illuminati's "Plunge Protection Team" calls for major Blue Chip companies to flood the market with an excess of stock purchases in order to maintain the illusion of a sound U.S. economy. Meanwhile, corporate bankruptcy, unemployment figures, bank failures, housing foreclosures, etc., are escalating. There are other factors involved in the rationale for why the PPT would be implemented at key fractal junctures, and the Illuminati's concern over the author's timeline forecast is probably low on the list, but when credible information becomes available to a public made frightened and insecure about the future, and trillions of dollars are at stake, direct correlations between forecasts of future stock market events which I have published, and the subsequent reaction in financial markets, do become obvious.

12) *Is there ever an endpoint in the fractal configuration beyond which no further price movement is possible?*

That may occur in the short-term, such as when a corporation becomes bankrupt and its stock declines to near zero. In the long-term view of the U.S. economy, as measured by the stock indices, an ultimate endpoint could only be reached in the event of a total global financial collapse. This would involve major repercussions as defined in the prophetic record of the Book of Daniel (Chapters 4, 7-9, 11,12), the gospels of Matthew (Chapter 24) and Luke (Chapter 21), and the Book of Revelation. These sources reference a culminating endtime apocalyptic scenario that would require a terminal point in the U.S. and global financial banking system. At present, according to my Fractal Analysis applied to the U.S. stock indices, the endpoint of the fractal configuration appears to be either 2020 or 2051. Any continuation beyond that date would start a new millennial cycle.

13) *What is your investment recommendation for the difficult financial times that you are forecasting?*

My recommendation is not to invest for the long-term, but only to hold paper on a year by year, or even month by month basis, while implementing a shorting strategy. Any long-term positions are doomed to bear the consequences of the trap being set by the world controllers who hope to lure and entice you to your own demise. Especially in consideration of sudden bank closings and consequent inaccessible cash for withdrawal, having the ability to instantly convert cash into needed tangible hard assets will preserve wealth and do much to maintain your continued survival.

14) The market *is being artificially inflated by government stimulus and high speed computer algorithms, which are far from the natural buying and selling pressure that should normally dictate the market. How does your work take into account these abnormalities that have for the most part failed all traditional technical analysis studies? It looks as if the markets are currently being dictated by robot computers and not human beings. Is this perception correct?*

While it is possible to *warp* or *temporarily disrupt* the progression of a naturally-occurring phenomenon, such as the fractal configuration and its inherent symmetry, it is not possible to indefinitely forestall its completion. When applying the study to past stock market history, what you see is a consistent fulfillment of the expected fractal structure. The exceptions that you have noted are incorporated into the overall pattern by allowing for the possibility of a continuation or aborted trend. But even this is subject to the rules governing the objectively derived fractal construct. Computer robots and algorithms were programmed by human beings, so the configuration is not divorced from the expected order. While it may seem from a limited timeline perspective that the geometry has been superseded and violated, in a long-term view it remains true to form. Discerning the malformed pattern of the fractal iteration – when resulting from factors such as you have mentioned – is subject to certain definitive rules and characteristics. If, for example, a continuation trend has been identified in the broad market, there are fractal analytic criteria that can be applied to precisely locate the eventual termination point of that trend.

Friday, May 7, 2010

Dow plummets by almost 1,000 points

1 p.m:
10,797.68

Day ends with loss of 'only' 348 points as 'unusual' trades made in error suspected as trigger for dive

2:30 p.m:
10,590.83,
down 277.29

4 p.m:
10,520.32,
down 347.80

By Adam Shell and Matt Krantz
USA TODAY

NEW YORK — In a late-day plunge eerily reminiscent of famous Wall Street stock market meltdowns in 1987 and the fall of 2008, the Dow Jones industrials nosedived almost 1,000 points Wednesday in a volatile day that began with heavy selling on Greek debt fears and was followed by a waterfall decline that was allegedly caused by erroneous trades and "unusual trading activity."

Cover story In a roughly 15-minute span that began around 2:30 p.m. on Wall Street, the Dow, which was already down almost 300 points, suffered the bulk of its biggest-ever intraday dive, falling as much as 998.50 points, or 9.2%, to 9869.62. The violent drop was followed by a rebound nearly as steep, with the Dow finishing down 347.80 points, or 3.2%, to 10,502.32.

The fast-and-furious drop caught traders off guard, sparking a vicious rumor mill, as there was no apparent news event to spark such a sudden plunge. While it was occurring, Andy Brooks, a trader at T. Rowe Price, guessed that it was a so-called "fat finger" trade, a term used to describe a trade that is entered incorrectly by human hands. "I have no idea why it happened; when it falls that far and fast and bounces back that quickly, you figure it's an error or tech snafu," Brooks said.

It turns out the veteran trader's suspicions were on target. Some unusual trades are believed to have been made in error — in well-known, big-name stocks such as Procter & Gamble, which dropped 37% in the blink of an

Please see COVER STORY next page ▶

By the numbers

On Thursday, the Dow Jones industrial average had one of the most turbulent trading days in its history and suffered its biggest intraday loss.

▶ Thursday's intraday trade loss: **998.50**
▶ Thursday's intraday percentage loss: **9.2%**
▶ Thursday's point loss: **347.80**
▶ Thursday's percentage loss: **3.2%**
▶ Percentage loss since record close of 14,164.53 on Oct. 9, 2007: **25.7%**
▶ Point loss over past three days: **631.51**
▶ Percentage loss over past three days: **5.7%**
▶ Largest three-day point loss since: **November 2008**
▶ Largest three-day percentage loss since: **March 2009**
▶ Percentage gain this year: **0.9%**

Sources: The Associated Press, Dow Jones & Co.

2:46 p.m:
9870 — a 998.50-point loss on the day that was the Dow's largest intraday trade loss ever.

Modern computerized trading programs can exaggerate but not eliminate the expected fractal configuration.

SAMPLE TRADING RECORDS
USING FRACTAL ANALYSIS

SAMPLE #1

Starting Amount: $350
9 Weeks, 8 Trades, $12,933 Profit, 3695% Return
Ending Balance: $13,283.01

AMERITRADE Apex

(2) New Messages | Help Center | Contact Us | Open New Acco

Shortcuts   Get Quotes Symbol lookup   **Search**   Acco
Select...   ex: MSFT, +IBMAT   Go   ex: Margin trading   Go

Home | **Accounts** | Trade | Research & Ideas | Trading Tools | Planning & Retirement | Client Services

Balances & Positions | Portfolio | Gain/Loss | Watch Lists | **History & Statements** | Deposit/Withdraw | Cash Mgmt

Mo : Dec 22 2008 11:55:18 AM EST   *NEW* Questions? Ask Ted. | Printer-friendly page | Page help

History & Statements

	Date/Time ▲	Description	Amount	Net Cash Balance
Start	03/28/2008 13:14:11	WIRE INCOMING	350.00	$350.00
	03/31/2008 00:00:01	MONEY MARKET PURCHASE (MMDA1)	0.00	$350.00
	03/31/2008 00:00:01	MONEY MARKET PURCHASE	-350.00	$0.00
	04/10/2008 15:03:26	Bought 1 SWOPQ @ 3.3	-340.74	-$340.74
	04/11/2008 03:52:32	MONEY MARKET REDEMPTION	340.74	$0.00
	04/11/2008 03:52:43	MONEY MARKET REDEMPTION (MMDA1)	0.00	$0.00
	04/11/2008 15:58:06	Sold 1 SWOPQ @ 4.2	409.26	$409.26
	04/14/2008 00:00:01	MONEY MARKET PURCHASE (MMDA1)	0.00	$409.26
	04/14/2008 00:00:01	MONEY MARKET PURCHASE	-409.26	$0.00
	04/17/2008 15:56:19	Bought 1 XAVQP @ 3.8	-390.74	-$390.74
	04/24/2008 10:26:57	Sold 1 XAVQP @ 11.3	1,119.26	$1,119.26
	04/24/2008 13:15:26	Bought 2 SWOEP @ 5.4	-1,091.49	$27.77
	04/25/2008 07:16:52	MONEY MARKET PURCHASE	-27.77	$0.00
	04/25/2008 07:17:13	MONEY MARKET PURCHASE (MMDA1)	0.00	$0.00
	04/30/2008 22:01:07	MONEY MARKET INTEREST (MMDA1)	0.00	$0.00
	05/16/2008 13:18:25	Sold 2 SWOEP @ 8.9	1,768.51	$1,768.51
	05/16/2008 14:35:34	Bought 2 XAVRQ @ 7	-1,411.49	$357.02

05/19/2008 00:00:01	MONEY MARKET PURCHASE (MMDA1)	0.00	$357.02
05/19/2008 00:00:01	MONEY MARKET PURCHASE	-357.02	$0.00
05/20/2008 11:07:22	Bought 1 XAVRP @ 3.9	-400.74	-$400.74
05/21/2008 02:40:11	MONEY MARKET REDEMPTION	400.74	$0.00
05/21/2008 02:40:24	MONEY MARKET REDEMPTION (MMDA1)	0.00	$0.00
05/29/2008 12:55:41	Sold 2 XAVRQ @ 10	1,988.51	$1,988.51
05/29/2008 12:55:44	Sold 1 XAVRP @ 7	689.26	$2,677.77
05/30/2008 02:44:56	MONEY MARKET PURCHASE	-2,677.77	$0.00
05/30/2008 02:45:24	MONEY MARKET PURCHASE (MMDA1)	0.00	$0.00
05/30/2008 15:56:50	Bought 1 XAVFQ @ 4.4	-450.74	-$450.74
05/30/2008 21:48:56	MONEY MARKET INTEREST (MMDA1)	0.00	-$450.74
06/02/2008 00:00:01	MONEY MARKET REDEMPTION	450.74	$0.00
06/03/2008 15:39:11	Bought 1 XAVFQ @ 3.2	-330.74	-$330.74
06/04/2008 02:40:53	MONEY MARKET REDEMPTION	330.74	$0.00
06/04/2008 02:41:10	MONEY MARKET REDEMPTION (MMDA1)	0.00	$0.00
06/04/2008 11:33:36	Bought 2 XAVFQ @ 2.4	-491.49	-$491.49
06/04/2008 11:53:34	Bought 1 XAVFQ @ 2.3	-240.74	-$732.23
06/04/2008 13:36:34	Bought 1 XAVFQ @ 2.55	-265.74	-$997.97
06/04/2008 14:12:13	Bought 1 XAVFQ @ 2.5	-260.74	-$1,258.71
06/04/2008 15:09:13	Bought 3 XAVFQ @ 2.1	-642.24	-$1,900.95
06/06/2008 13:34:31	Sold 10 XAVFQ @ 5.2	5,182.51	$5,182.51
06/06/2008 13:45:38	Bought 2 XAVRQ @ 4.8	-971.49	$4,211.02
06/06/2008 15:02:46	Bought 2 XAVRQ @ 4.6	-931.49	$3,279.53
06/09/2008 00:00:01	MONEY MARKET PURCHASE (MMDA1)	0.00	$3,279.53
06/09/2008 00:00:01	MONEY MARKET PURCHASE	-3,279.53	$0.00
06/09/2008 12:51:55	Bought 4 XAVRQ @ 4	-1,612.99	-$1,612.99
06/09/2008 15:54:49	Bought 2 XAVRQ @ 4.7	-951.49	-$2,564.48
06/10/2008 03:00:47	MONEY MARKET REDEMPTION	2,564.48	$0.00
06/10/2008 03:01:24	MONEY MARKET REDEMPTION (MMDA1)	0.00	$0.00
06/10/2008 14:51:20	Sold 10 XAVRQ @ 9.7	9,682.51	$9,682.51
06/11/2008 02:42:08	MONEY MARKET PURCHASE	-9,682.51	$0.00
06/11/2008 02:42:15	MONEY MARKET PURCHASE (MMDA1)	0.00	$0.00
06/11/2008 11:12:51	Bought 14 XAVRQ @ 7.4	-10,380.49	-$10,380.49
06/11/2008 14:57:57	Sold 14 XAVRQ @ 7.8	10,899.51	$519.02
06/12/2008 03:18:30	MONEY MARKET PURCHASE	-519.02	$0.00
06/12/2008 03:19:09	MONEY MARKET PURCHASE (MMDA1)	0.00	$0.00
06/12/2008 11:03:14	Bought 15 XAVFO @ 3	-4,521.24	-$4,521.24
06/12/2008 11:37:51	Bought 21 XAVFO @ 2.9	-6,115.74	-$10,636.98
06/13/2008 02:41:39	MONEY MARKET REDEMPTION	10,636.98	$0.00
06/13/2008 02:41:59	MONEY MARKET REDEMPTION (MMDA1)	0.00	$0.00
06/13/2008 11:50:45	Sold 36 XAVFO @ 3.7	13,283.01	$13,283.01

End

SAMPLE #2

Starting Amount: $310.74
1 Week, 4 Trades, $3744 Profit, 1205% Return
Ending Balance: $4,036.26

History & Statements

Date/Time ▲	Description	Amount	Net Cash Balance
11/25/2008 16:46:51	WIRE INCOMING	292.00	$292.00
11/26/2008 03:09:42	MONEY MARKET PURCHASE	-292.00	$0.00
11/26/2008 03:09:56	MONEY MARKET PURCHASE (MMDA1)	0.00	$0.00
11/28/2008 21:35:17	MONEY MARKET INTEREST (MMDA1)	0.00	$0.00
12/05/2008 11:04:13	Bought 1 XAULR @ 3	-310.74	-$310.74
12/08/2008 00:00:01	MONEY MARKET REDEMPTION (MMDA1)	0.00	-$310.74
12/08/2008 00:00:01	MONEY MARKET REDEMPTION	310.74	$0.00
12/08/2008 14:54:45	Sold 1 XAULR @ 9.1	899.26	$899.26
12/08/2008 15:03:56	Bought 1 XAUXR @ 3.9	-400.74	$498.52
12/09/2008 02:53:58	MONEY MARKET PURCHASE	-498.52	$0.00
12/09/2008 02:54:15	MONEY MARKET PURCHASE (MMDA1)	0.00	$0.00
12/09/2008 14:14:10	Bought 1 XAUXR @ 3.2	-330.74	-$330.74
12/09/2008 15:26:47	Sold 2 XAUXR @ 3.5	688.51	$357.77
12/09/2008 15:53:40	Bought 2 XAVLT @ 4	-811.49	-$453.72
12/10/2008 02:56:02	MONEY MARKET REDEMPTION	453.72	$0.00
12/10/2008 02:56:19	MONEY MARKET REDEMPTION (MMDA1)	0.00	$0.00
12/11/2008 10:09:57	Sold 2 XAVLT @ 13.5	2,688.51	$2,688.51
12/11/2008 11:08:12	Bought 2 XAVXB @ 5.6	-1,131.49	$1,557.02
12/11/2008 11:48:22	Bought 2 XAVXB @ 5.3	-1,071.49	$485.53
12/11/2008 12:29:21	Bought 1 XAVXB @ 5.2	-530.74	-$45.21
12/11/2008 15:21:56	Sold 5 XAVXB @ 8.1	4,036.26	$3,991.05

Start

End

SAMPLE #3

Starting Amount: $48,300
10 Days, 12 Trades, $104,700 Profit, 217% Return
Ending Balance: $152,999.39

	Date/Time ▾	Description	Amount	Net Cash Balance
End	06/12/2009 11:59:09	Sold 10 XAVRJ @ 6.2	6,187.50	*152,999.39*
	06/12/2009 11:57:01	Sold 100 XAVRJ @ 6.3	62,920.00	---
	06/12/2009 11:51:04	Sold 50 XAVRJ @ 6.5	32,457.50	---
	06/11/2009 15:32:00	Bought 40 XAVRJ @ 4.4	-17,635.00	---
	06/11/2009 14:58:02	Bought 40 XAVRJ @ 3.9	-15,635.00	---
	06/11/2009 14:39:33	Bought 40 XAVRJ @ 4.2	-16,835.00	---
	06/11/2009 14:05:01	Bought 40 XAVRJ @ 4	-16,035.00	---
	06/10/2009 15:46:21	Sold 260 XAVRJ @ 4.7	122,000.00	---
	06/09/2009 13:17:12	Bought 260 XAVRJ @ 4.5	-117,200.00	---
	06/08/2009 15:42:01	Sold 411 XAVFL @ 2	81,886.75	---
	06/08/2009 13:08:16	Bought 60 XAVFL @ 1.5	-9,050.00	---
	06/08/2009 12:14:12	Bought 61 XAVFL @ 1.2	-7,370.75	---
	06/08/2009 09:43:47	Bought 200 XAVFL @ 1.3	-26,155.00	---
	06/05/2009 15:56:18	Bought 65 XAVFL @ 2.25	-14,678.75	---
	06/05/2009 14:40:44	Bought 25 XAVFL @ 2.2	-5,523.75	---
	06/05/2009 11:15:38	Sold 125 XAVFL @ 2.8	34,901.25	---
	06/05/2009 10:29:16	Bought 50 XAVFL @ 2.2	-11,042.50	---
	06/05/2009 10:04:33	Bought 50 XAVFL @ 2.6	-13,042.50	---
	06/05/2009 09:44:01	Bought 25 XAVFL @ 2.9	-7,273.75	---
	06/04/2009 13:48:18	Sold 150 XAVFL @ 5.3	79,382.50	---
	06/03/2009 13:47:09	Bought 25 XAVFL @ 2.4	-6,023.75	---
	06/03/2009 13:18:36	Bought 25 XAVFL @ 2.9	-7,273.75	---
	06/03/2009 12:19:30	Bought 50 XAVFL @ 3.4	-17,042.50	---
	06/03/2009 11:34:05	Bought 25 XAVFL @ 4.2	-10,523.75	---
	06/03/2009 10:26:17	Bought 25 XAVFL @ 4.5	-11,273.75	---
	06/03/2009 09:56:11	Sold 170 XAVRJ @ 3.7	62,767.50	---
	06/02/2009 14:15:44	Bought 50 XAVRJ @ 2.3	-11,542.50	---
	06/02/2009 11:01:40	Bought 50 XAVRJ @ 2.5	-12,542.50	---
	06/01/2009 13:55:45	Bought 70 XAVRJ @ 2.9	-20,357.50	---
	05/29/2009 23:33:40	FREE BALANCE INTEREST ADJUSTMENT	0.79	---
Start	05/26/2009 19:41:24	CLIENT REQUESTED ELECTRONIC FUNDING RECEIPT (FUNDS NOW)	48,300.00	---

SAMPLE #4

Starting Amount: $4000
4 Weeks, 8 Trades, $13,999 Profit, 350% Return
Ending Balance: $17,999.26

	Date/Time ▲	Description	Amount	Net Cash Balance
	06/30/2009 19:24:56	CLIENT REQUESTED ELECTRONIC FUNDING RECEIPT (FUNDS NOW)	4,000.00	$4,000.00
	06/30/2009 21:16:20	MONEY MARKET INTEREST (MMDA1)	0.00	$4,000.00
	06/30/2009 21:34:05	FREE BALANCE INTEREST ADJUSTMENT	0.01	$4,000.01
	07/01/2009 03:39:26	MONEY MARKET PURCHASE	-4,000.01	$0.00
	07/01/2009 03:39:34	MONEY MARKET PURCHASE (MMDA1)	0.00	$0.00
Start	07/07/2009 11:56:47	Bought 11 XAVGG @ 3.6	-3,978.24	-$3,978.24
	07/07/2009 15:44:02	Sold 11 XAVGG @ 3.4	3,721.76	-$256.48
	07/08/2009 02:28:22	MONEY MARKET REDEMPTION	256.48	$0.00
	07/08/2009 02:28:40	MONEY MARKET REDEMPTION (MMDA1)	0.00	$0.00
	07/08/2009 11:06:32	Bought 16 XAVGG @ 2.35	-3,781.99	-$3,781.99
	07/09/2009 14:47:53	Sold 16 XAVGG @ 2.4	3,818.01	$3,818.01
	07/10/2009 02:33:07	MONEY MARKET PURCHASE	-3,818.01	$0.00
	07/10/2009 02:33:13	MONEY MARKET PURCHASE (MMDA1)	0.00	$0.00
	07/21/2009 15:52:51	Bought 4 XAVTI @ 5.4	-2,172.99	-$2,172.99
	07/22/2009 02:29:38	MONEY MARKET REDEMPTION	2,172.99	$0.00
	07/22/2009 02:29:49	MONEY MARKET REDEMPTION (MMDA1)	0.00	$0.00
	07/22/2009 10:01:43	Sold 4 XAVTI @ 5.5	2,187.01	$2,187.01
	07/22/2009 13:58:08	Bought 1 XAVTI @ 4.6	-470.74	$1,716.27
	07/22/2009 13:58:10	Bought 7 XAVTI @ 4.7	-3,305.24	-$1,588.97
	07/22/2009 15:03:04	Sold 8 XAVTI @ 4.8	3,824.01	$2,235.04
	07/23/2009 02:26:51	MONEY MARKET PURCHASE	-2,235.04	$0.00
	07/23/2009 02:27:00	MONEY MARKET PURCHASE (MMDA1)	0.00	$0.00
	07/23/2009 09:56:26	Bought 8 XAVTI @ 4.8	-3,855.99	-$3,855.99
	07/24/2009 02:30:34	MONEY MARKET REDEMPTION	3,855.99	$0.00
	07/24/2009 02:30:42	MONEY MARKET REDEMPTION (MMDA1)	0.00	$0.00
	07/28/2009 11:20:51	Sold 8 XAVTI @ 7.7	6,144.01	$6,144.01
	07/28/2009 11:45:34	Bought 15 XAVHI @ 4	-6,021.24	$122.77

07/28/2009	12:03:10	Sold 15 XAVHI @ 4.2	6,278.76	$6,401.53
07/29/2009	02:40:57	MONEY MARKET PURCHASE	-6,401.53	$0.00
07/29/2009	02:41:28	MONEY MARKET PURCHASE (MMDA1)	0.00	$0.00
07/29/2009	10:45:48	Bought 20 XAVHI @ 3.2	-6,424.99	-$6,424.99
07/30/2009	08:16:07	MONEY MARKET REDEMPTION	6,424.99	$0.00
07/30/2009	08:16:13	MONEY MARKET REDEMPTION (MMDA1)	0.00	$0.00
07/31/2009	14:27:19	Sold 20 XAVHI @ 8.3	16,575.01	$16,575.01
08/03/2009	10:30:30	Bought 26 XAVTJ @ 3.8	-9,909.49	-$9,909.49
08/04/2009	02:30:59	MONEY MARKET REDEMPTION	9,909.49	$0.00
08/04/2009	02:31:31	MONEY MARKET REDEMPTION (MMDA11)	0.00	$0.00
08/05/2009	09:34:40	Bought 15 XAVTJ @ 4.2	-6,321.24	-$6,321.24
08/05/2009	09:34:40	Bought 15 XAVTJ @ 4.2	6,321.24	$0.00
08/05/2009	09:34:40	Bought 15 XAVTJ @ 4.2	-6,321.24	-$6,321.24
08/05/2009	13:26:25	Sold 41 XAVTJ @ 4.4	17,999.26	$11,678.02
08/05/2009	13:26:25	Sold 41 XAVTJ @ 4.4	-17,999.26	-$6,321.24
08/05/2009	13:26:25	Sold 41 XAVTJ @ 4.4	17,999.26	$11,678.02

SAMPLE #5

Starting Amount: $2,076.11
7 Weeks, 7 Trades, $12,191 Profit, 587% Return
Ending Balance: $14,267.38

---

(0) New Messages | Help Center | Contact Us | Open New Acco

AMERITRADE   Shortcuts   Get Quotes Symbol lookup   Search   Accc
                 Select...   ex: MSFT. +IBMAT Go   ex: Margin trading   Go

Home | **Accounts** | Trade | Research & Ideas | Trading Tools | Planning & Retirement | Education | Client !

Balances & Positions | Portfolio | Gain/Loss | Watch Lists | **History & Statements** | Deposit/Withdraw | Cash Mgmt

Mon Dec 06 2010 11:44:16 AM EST   *NEW* Questions? Ask Ted. | Printer-friendly page | Page help

History & Statements

	Date/Time ▲	Description	Amount ▫	Net Cash Balance
	10/07/2010 12:19:06	Sold 10 XAU Oct 16 2010 195.0 Put @ 2	1,982.51	2,076.11
Start	10/07/2010 12:44:46	Bought 5 XAU Oct 16 2010 200.0 Call @ 4.1	-2,063.74	12.37
	10/08/2010 13:14:29	Sold 5 XAU Oct 16 2010 200.0 Call @ 6.6	3,286.26	3,298.63
	10/15/2010 15:56:27	Bought 1 XAU Nov 20 2010 210.0 Call @ 6.1	-620.74	2,677.89
	10/15/2010 15:59:41	Bought 4 XAU Nov 20 2010 210.0 Call @ 6.4	-2,572.99	104.90
	10/29/2010 22:39:29	FREE BALANCE INTEREST ADJUSTMENT	0.03	104.93
	11/04/2010 14:48:30	Sold 5 XAU Nov 20 2010 210.0 Call @ 7.5	3,736.26	3,841.19
	11/05/2010 10:52:55	Bought 9 XAU Nov 20 2010 215.0 Put @ 4.2	-3,796.74	44.45
	11/10/2010 10:42:00	Sold 9 XAU Nov 20 2010 215.0 Put @ 5	4,483.26	4,527.71
	11/15/2010 10:09:43	Bought 10 XAU Nov 20 2010 215.0 Put @ 4.5	-4,517.49	10.22
	11/16/2010 10:12:03	Sold 10 XAU Nov 20 2010 215.0 Put @ 7.1	7,082.51	7,092.73
	11/16/2010 11:28:44	Bought 10 XAU Dec 18 2010 210.0 Call @ 7	-7,017.49	75.24
	11/18/2010 12:29:35	Sold 10 XAU Dec 18 2010 210.0 Call @ 9.4	9,382.51	9,457.75
	11/22/2010 14:09:08	Bought 12 XAU Dec 18 2010 215.0 Put @ 7.8	-9,378.99	78.76
	11/26/2010 10:11:45	Sold 12 XAU Dec 18 2010 215.0 Put @ 8	9,581.01	9,659.77
	11/26/2010 11:29:51	Bought 15 XAU Dec 18 2010 210.0 Call @ 6.4	-9,621.24	38.53
	11/30/2010 22:04:47	FREE BALANCE INTEREST ADJUSTMENT	0.09	38.62
End	12/01/2010 12:45:13	Sold 15 XAU Dec 18 2010 210.0 Call @ 9.5	14,228.76	14,267.38

The fear of the LORD is the beginning of wisdom.

— Psalm 111:10

So shall the knowledge of wisdom be unto thy soul: when thou hast found it, then there shall be a reward, and thy expectation shall not be cut off.

— Proverb 24:14

For by wise counsel thou shalt make thy war: and in multitude of counsellors there is safety.

— Proverb 24:6

What the Illuminati Globalists **FEAR** the most ...

The Authorized 1611 King James Bible is the ONLY Word of God.

There is one body, and one Spirit, even as ye are called in one hope of your calling; One Lord, one faith, one baptism, One God and Father of all ... (Ephesians 4:4-6).

There is Only ONE Word of God ...
Jesus Christ,

his name is called the Word of God (Revelation 19:13), *the way, the truth, and the life* (John 14:6), *the sword of the Spirit* (Ephesians 6:17), *quick, and powerful, and sharper than any twoedged sword* (Hebrews 4:12). *In the beginning was the Word, and the Word was with God, and the Word was God. The same was in the beginning with God. All things were made by him; and without him was not any thing made that was made. In him was life; and the life was the light of men. And the light shineth in darkness; and the darkness comprehended it not* (John 1:1-5).

Jesus Christ is God, One God, the *spoken* **Word of God**; His 1611 King James Bible is One Word, the *written* **Word of God**, Jesus Christ.

Sanctify them through thy truth: thy word is truth (John 17:17).

For I testify unto every man that heareth the words of the prophecy of this book, If any man shall add unto these things, God shall add unto him the plagues that are written in this book. And if any man shall take away from the words of the book of this prophecy, God shall take away his part out of the book of life, and out of the holy city, and from the things which are written in this book (Revelation 22:18,19).

PREVIEW OF COMPANION BOOK
TO FRACTAL TRADING

When Will the Illuminati Crash the Stock Market?
An Insider's Look at the Elite Satanic Luciferians
Who Dictate the Rise and Fall of Global Economies
376 pages

The world's financial elite are spraying us with poisonous Chemtrails; they're force-injecting our children with deadly vaccines; U.S. sovereignty has been destroyed and replaced by a shadow world government. This is not science fiction, but reality, and it's happening NOW.

Are we headed for a
GLOBAL ECONOMIC COLLAPSE?

Most people realize that it will *eventually* occur, so the only question of any significance is WHEN? Can the precise timing, even the very year, quarter, and month, be predicted far in advance? The many *scorners* will say, "No!", but the Word of God says: *A scorner seeketh wisdom, and findeth it not ... and the scorners delight in their scorning, and fools hate knowledge (Proverbs 14:6;1:22).* Economists and financial market professionals have traditionally relied upon information that has consistently proven to be *wrong*.

The collapse and political-economic restructuring of Western Civilization is imminent, and one man knows when it will occur ... and what happens *next*.

After *crashing down* New York City's World Trade Towers on September 11, 2001, the next major "terrorist act" staged by the global supra-government (Illuminati) will be the *crashing down* of the U.S. and Global Stock Markets.

Imagine the following scenario: Another government-engineered terrorist attack against its citizenry precipitates the ultimate economic crash, devastating the currency and financial infrastructure of America and the rest of the world. A new international President (Antichrist) emerges from the shadows to stabilize the global economy by unifying world currencies into a single monetary unit. Suddenly, every person on earth is thrust into making the most important decision of their life: *"Do I take the microchip* Mark of the Beast – *Yes* or *No?"* Now, don't just imagine it, but *know* this will most certainly occur, and *WHEN*.

The significance of identifying the end point of the U.S. economy, as designated by a major economic indicator such as the Dow Jones Industrial Average, is vastly more far reaching than merely announcing the end of American prosperity. The implications and consequences to follow are of world historical and Biblical proportions, since this forecast not only precedes the termination of U.S. sovereignty as an independent nation-state, but of much greater relevance, portends the completion of the seventh millennial epoch of the existence of mankind on planet Earth. It sets in motion the prophetic time clock that counts down the remaining moments until the return of Jesus Christ, and His final Judgment of the inhabitants of the world. It speaks to the key events immediately prior to that 7000 year prophesy, including the appearance and reign of the Antichrist (World President/Dictator), his oppressive global government (New World Order), and the computerized mass enslavement of a microchipped world population (Mark of the Beast technology). It presages the final Armageddon script of war between two worlds: the kingdom of Satan's wicked earthly human government defeated by the righteous government of God's heavenly host (Revelation 19:11-21).

The incident which occurred in New York City on September 11, 2001 was a planned act of war used as a pretext for initiating the "War on Terrorism" *against the American people*. It was contrived in order to create anti-Constitutional laws to forfeit citizen's

Constitutional rights, increase domestic security, and facilitate loss of U.S. sovereignty in preparation for instituting a global Police State world government. The staged event was planned by a supra-national small group of Luciferian dynasties, mediated by the CIA, and allowed to occur by the U.S. government puppet regime. It was intended to terrorize the American people into sacrificing their Constitutional rights in exchange for "peace and safety" from the ubiquitous "terrorists." (The *only* terrorist is *the government* – at all levels: Supra-national, Federal, State, local.) The U.S. criminal elite also hoped to declare a State of Emergency (Martial Law: impose military rule over the civilian population), but "only" managed to murder 3000 innocent people. The terrorism was planned 15 years in advance and was scheduled on that occultically significant 9/11 date because the Luciferian globalists believed they would derive satanic power to covertly deceive U.S. citizens into an unquestioned acceptance of the bold lie that "the Arab terrorists did it". The real reason for blaming the "Arabs" was to gain public support for U.S. military aggression in the Middle East in order to control Iraqi oil reserves and Afghanistan poppy opium production.

Mass human enslavement by a newly installed global government is about to be activated upon crashing of the U.S. stock market. Militarization of local police departments (officially made effective August 2009), FEMA death camp "Re-education Centers" (already constructed throughout America), dictatorial post 9/11 legislation (Patriot Acts 1, 2; Homeland Security, etc.) are in place and ready to be implemented *against the U.S. population.*

What nearly everyone fails to realize is this is not a distant prophesy in the unforeseeable future, but a *current event*, a very real historical fact *about to transpire*. To the glory of God, the author is one of the few people in the world who understands its imminence relative to the present, and is perhaps the only person to objectively quantify that occurrence to within a specific narrow interval of time.

This book is an accurate chronicle of the unfolding *future timeline* of history, tracing the advance and sudden fall of today's

America and the rest of the modern world. The author's in-depth understanding of the subtle nuances implicit in that cosmic denouement casts new and revealing light upon a subject that is seldom clearly understood.

BOOK ORDERING

The following books can be ordered online from:
bn.com or amazon.com

Any other websites are unapproved and unauthorized.
These titles can also be purchased direct from retail bookstores.

___ The Great Deception

___ The Coming of Wisdom (sequel to The Great Deception)

___ Fools Paradise: *The Spiritual Implications of Gambling*

___ Seven Who Dared

___ The Criminal Fraternity: *Servants of the Lie*

___ *When* Will the Illuminati Crash the Stock Market? *An Insider's Look at the Elite Satanic Luciferians Who Dictate the Rise and Fall of Global Economies*

___ Genesis 1:29 Diet: *Perfect Health without Doctors, Hospitals, or Pharmaceutical Drugs*

___ Fractal Trading: *Analyzing Financial Markets using Fractal Geometry and the Golden Ratio*

___ The Globalist's Agenda: *Design for a New World Order*

___ Everything is a Test: *How God Delivered Me from "Impossible" Situations*

soulesprit.com

Lightning Source UK Ltd.
Milton Keynes UK
UKOW05f1105160117
292169UK00001B/98/P